THE BIG BOOK OF JUST FOR GIRLS

D0514624

Kidsbooks®

Visit us at www.kidsbooks.com®

Search & Finds®, Mazes, Crosswords, How to Tips, and More!

Get ready for hours of fun—exclusively for girls! You'll love solving puzzles and learning cool fashion and girl tips along the way with The Big Book of Just for Girls!

If you get stumped on any of the puzzles, don't worry—we put the answers in the back of the book!

Girls of all ages will enjoy this activity book—anytime and anywhere. Start working your way through—there are lots of awesome activities just for girls!

Kidsbooks®

How To
TIPS
Be a Terrific Friend

Friends are fantastic! True friends are always there for you even when it seems like no one else cares. Follow these guidelines to make some new ones and keep your current ones.

JOIN THE WAGON!

Join a club or sign up for an after-school activity that interests you. You'll already have something in common with the other kids who are in it. Since you share the same interest—whether it's riding horses or painting—chances are you'll make a cool connection with the kids in the club.

TAKE A CLOSER LOOK!

If you'd like some new friends, look around you. Try to get to know a lot of people so you can find the ones with whom you really click. Don't be nervous or afraid—chances are the girls around you are looking for friends, too!

FEELINGS MATTER!

It's always good to consider other people's feelings. Good friends think about their pals' feelings at all times. They listen when their buds need them to, and they don't speak badly of their friends—ever.

TYPES OF HAIRSTYLES

It's always fun to play—and experiment— with your hair! Find these types of hairstyles in the word search below. Look up, down, backward, forward, and diagonally.

~~Bob~~	Curled	Long	Pixie	Short
Crimped	~~Layered~~	Perm	Shag	Updo

```
R C X A E K L E E E J L X L
J R I C T A E S C H Q B X U
U I F X Y P E S H U F W L U
P M B E U O S N G A Z D G P
B P R I Z M N N V E G U Y D
V E S A B F O P O C I P S O
D D I N B L Y J R C G E H Q
Z L N X A S U W Y E V W W T
A B J H I F B U Z O A X S R
L L B Q T P V A F M M M V Q O
B O Q W D R P U H U V R A H
B R G L Z I S C I N R R L S
D L Y D D E L R U C R F V D
P E R M D T R O E Z C X H G
```

Answer on page 268

What's Your Style?

Sporty · Classic · Runway

1. You see a new pair of sneakers at the mall. What do you do?
- **a** – Buy them! My old pair is falling apart. (1)
- **b** – I'll get them if I like the color. Sneakers always come in handy. (2)
- **c** – Keep moving–you'll never see me in sneakers! (3)

2. After school you can be found:
- **a** – Polishing an article for the school's newspaper. (2)
- **b** – Practicing my lines for the school play. (3)
- **c** – Running warm-up laps on the track. (1)

3. What's your favorite way to wear your hair?
- **a** – Straightened and sleek, with a sparkly clip on one side. (3)
- **b** – Up in a ponytail and out of the way! (1)
- **c** – Either down or up, but with a little wave to keep things interesting. (2)

4. What's your dream vacation destination?
- **a** – Paris, splitting my time between museums and shopping! (3)
- **b** – Cairo, to see amazing ruins and explore the exotic streets. (2)
- **c** – Grand Canyon National Park. Hiking my way to the bottom would be a blast! (1)

5. Which breed of dog do you like the best?
- **a** – Border collie–they're fast, smart, and always willing to leap for a Frisbee. (1)
- **b** – Golden retriever–they have beautiful coats and aren't afraid to go for a run. (2)
- **c** – Pomeranian–they're small, fluffy, and fit right in a lap! (3)

Sporty 5-8 points

Your style is Sporty. You prefer sneakers to flats, a ponytail to curls, and are most likely a very active person. You keep it simple and fun!

Classic 9-11 points

Your style is Classic. You're not overly flashy, but you like to keep things coordinated. Your outfits are planned down to the smallest accessories, and you love looking and feeling pretty!

Runway 12-15 points

Your style is Runway. You're the trendsetter at your school—you keep up with the latest fashions, and when it comes to hair, makeup, and accessorizing, you can't be beat!

Luscious Locks
Glamour
TIPS

Looking for a new 'do? Bad hair days are such a drag! If you're in a rut with your hair, try this easy DIY hairstyle.

STRAIGHT AND SLEEK

If your curly hair is unruly, try straightening it with these easy steps!

You'll need:
- Round hairbrush with a large barrel
- Hairdryer
- Hair clips
- Gloss serum

Comb towel-dried hair to remove any tangles or knots. Part hair into sections and clip up. Use your round hairbrush and hairdryer to dry the section that you are working on. Repeat with each section. Finish by spritzing a light gloss serum to add a touch of shine to your new straight 'do.

Kitten Maze

Follow the path from **Start** to **Finish** to help the girl find her lost kitten.

START

FINISH

I LOVE SCHOOL

Fill in the blanks to complete this silly story about school. Pick a NOUN, ADJECTIVE, or VERB from the word bank to place in a corresponding blank, or think of your own weird words!

Every day, I take a _pizza_ [NOUN] to school. My teacher gets

curly [ADJECTIVE] if we're late so I _explode_ [VERB] to my class.

My favorite class is _slime_ [NOUN]. Even though it's a _cute_ [ADJECTIVE]

class, I still like it. At noon, everyone _love_ [VERB] s to the cafeteria

to eat _finger painting_ [NOUN]. After lunch, the rest of the _crazy_ [ADJECTIVE] day

whizzes by—before I _bounce_ [VERB] it, I'm home!

WORD BANK

ADJECTIVES
~~cute~~   ugly
weird   ~~curly~~
angry   boring
hard   sweet
crazy

NOUNS
bus   limousine
~~pizza~~   rocket ship
flowers   rocket science
~~slime~~   finger painting
history

VERBS
jump   know
run   slither
dance   ~~explode~~
love   bounce
leap

ROCK
AND
ROLL

It's time to rock and roll! Can you find the two pictures that are exactly alike?

Answer on page 268

List your Sleepover Essentials

What better way to enjoy time with your friends than with a sleepover! Use these questions to help you pack for a night full of fun.

At whose place are you going to sleep over?

What was your favorite thing about your last sleepover?

What kind of fun games should you bring?

A sleepover is never complete without...

In addition to basic toiletries and clothes, what else should you pack?

Hip, Hop, Hooray!

Using the pictures below, complete this rebus puzzle about something that makes you want to say, "Hip, hop, hooray!"

– ICE +  – O

Arow   *Pear*

 – AR – W +  – AR

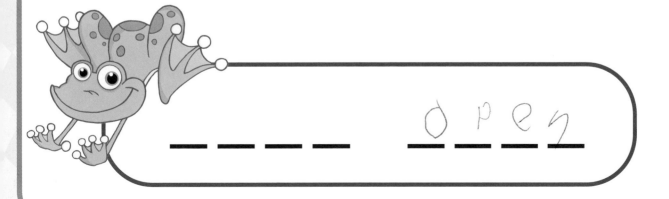

_ _ _ _   _ _ _ _

open

What Do You Want to Be When You Grow up?

You may have the right qualities for your dream job and not even know it! Take this quiz to find out what kind of job you might end up with.

	LIKE ME	NOT LIKE ME
1. I'm creative.		
2. I am a risk taker.		
3. My bedroom is usually a disaster.		
4. When I was little, I loved to play make-believe.		
5. I never throw anything away.		
6. English is my favorite subject in school.		
7. I'd rather make gifts than buy them.		
8. I like to enter the science fair every year.		
9. Even my sock drawers are neatly organized.		
10. I exercise as often as possible.		

11. History is my favorite subject.

12. I win a lot of trophies and certificates.

13. I never miss entering a talent show.

14. I read the newspaper at least once a week.

15. I get along with everybody.

Tally it up!

If you answered "Like Me" to four or more of these questions:
 # 1, 3, 4, 6, 7, 13, read **Careers A** below.

If you answered "Like Me" to four or more of these questions:
#2, 4, 5, 7, 8, 9, 12, read **Careers B** below.

If you answered "Like Me" to four or more of these questions:
#2, 5, 9, 11, 14, 15, read **Careers C** below.

Careers A

You have a true creative side! You are imaginative and innovative, and strongly drawn to the arts. Consider these careers: artist, entertainer, lawyer, musician, psychologist, teacher, and writer.

Careers B

You are destined for a future in business! You're organized, thoughtful, intelligent, and financially savvy. Possible career paths include advertising, business executive, CEO, company owner, finance, human resources, and sales.

Careers C

You are headed for politics! A natural-born leader, your strengths are in people management and problem-solving. Career choices might be business, community fundraising, and politics and government.

DANCING QUEEN

Are you a super seeker? Put your eyes to the test and see if you can find 10 differences between the picture on the top and the one on the bottom.

Answer on page 269

Write Your
Own Story

My sweet dreams are...

?

Let's Draw a
Golden Retriever Puppy

On a separate piece of paper, follow these simple steps using a pencil and an eraser.

1 Start out with these simple shapes to help define the proportions of the dog.

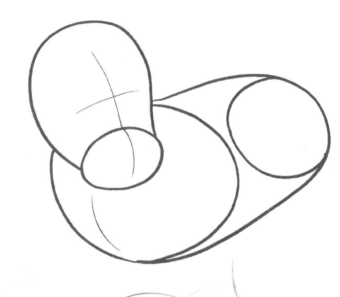

2 Next, sketch in the legs. The paws will start out as ovals and be adjusted later. Next, add the tail and start sketching the pup's face.

3 Tighten up your drawing by adding muscle tone and details. At this stage, you can add finer details such as fur and whiskers.

4 Your puppy is almost complete. Add some golden color and shading, and your puppy is ready to play and catch!

Recipes

CINNAMON-APPLE DAPPLE Snacks

To feel fit and fabulous, you need to get plenty of exercise and eat right! This snack can be prepared at home and carried to school for a treat at lunchtime or after class.

INGREDIENTS & DIRECTIONS

You'll need:

- 1 large apple
- Cinnamon
- Sugar
- Lemon juice
- A small plastic container

Ask your Mom or Dad* to help you peel and slice an apple into the small plastic container. Sprinkle your apple pieces with lemon juice (to keep them from turning brown). Then sprinkle them with a little cinnamon and sugar. Yum!

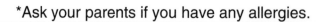

*Ask your parents if you have any allergies.

How To TIPS
Stop Gossiping

Gossiping can be exciting, but it can also hurt people's feelings. Keep these gossip guidelines in mind so you don't disrupt your friendship grooves.

BEING SILLY IS A-OK

If the gossip is silly and doesn't hurt anyone's feelings, it is okay to tell it to other people. If you've got a good scoop about one of your favorite Hollywood stars, then it's fine to share the dish with your pals.

BACK TALK

Don't talk about your friends behind their backs. Remember the saying: "What goes around, comes around."

ZIP IT!

Don't spread gossip that isn't nice, even if it is about someone you don't like. If you're tempted, just make believe that there's a little zipper on your mouth, keeping the gossip sealed away.

SQUASHING TIME

If someone is spreading a rumor about a friend, that's not okay. Try to stop the rumor before it really hurts your friend's feelings. If possible, find out who started it.

Sudoku
ROCKIN' TUNES

Rock out to some music and try to decode this sudoku. Fill in the empty squares so that each row, column, and square contains the numbers 1–9 only once.

			2	7		8		4
	7				4	6	2	
4		3	2	2	2		7	
7	8	6	2	4	1	5	2/8	2/8
4/4			7				3	
4				8		4		7
9	1	4	8		7	2		
3		2	4	5			7	1
		7	1	6	2	9	4	

Fabulous Facials
Glamour TIPS

Sometimes you need a little pick-me-up, and what better way to perk up than with a skin-soothing facial? Keep your face fresh and clean with this cool cucumber mask. Ask a parent before mixing up this facial mask.

COOL AS A CUCUMBER

Whip up this cooling facial mask if you have normal skin that needs a quick freshen up.

You'll need:

- ½ cup chopped cucumber
- ½ avocado
- 2 tablespoons powdered milk

Blend ingredients in a blender (ask a parent for help). Apply to your face and let set for 10 to 15 minutes. Rinse and pat dry.

Trip To The Mall Maze

Let's shop! Help this group of BFFs find the way to the mall by following the correct path through the maze. The correct path is made up of sale tags.

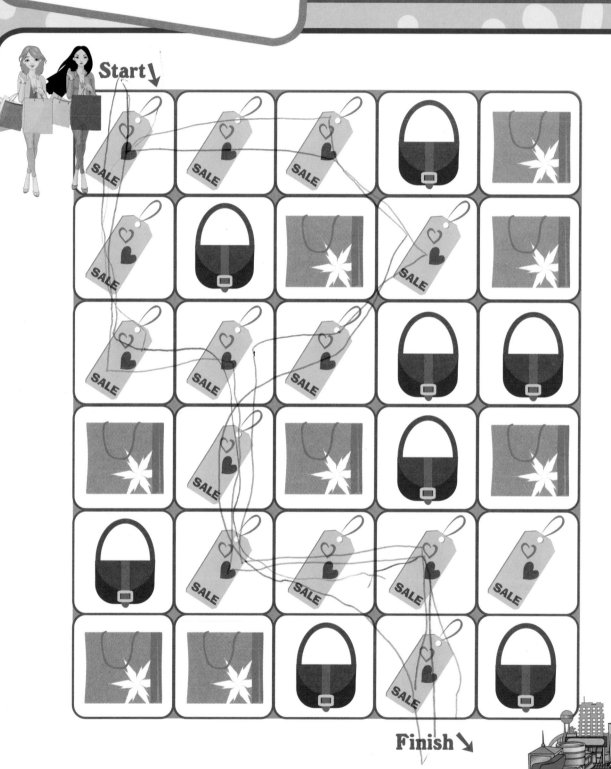

Start

Finish

Answer on page 269

FIT AND FABULOUS

It's good to stay in shape, and there are lots of fun exercises to keep you fit and fabulous. Find these types of exercises in the word search below. Look up, down, backward, forward, and diagonally.

Aerobics	Cardio	Pilates	Stretching	Tennis
Bike	Dance	Run	Swim	Yoga

```
N Q R F C S A G O Y T I B H
F O F A E C U I L S E D S I
A L S A C E D Q S A B J P F
H O M S N R K C D T P D A D
W S E T A L I P G U I M G S
O V O C D B I K E R O P G T
H E O S O A N U R X M E D R
Y H T R O L B E A E A T A E
S B E S F W S O I E E B M T
T A N R Z Z F T U G C Z P C
P N N N G S G R R B A X R H
A H I W H T Y O D P Y F X I
J W S W I M K I L N N A Q N
R G P I M U Z O F D H D M G
```

Answer on page 269

PRECIOUS ANIMALS

Use the clues about ponies and horses to complete this crossword puzzle.

DOWN
1. Name for a professional horse rider
2. Small horse
4. You put this seat on a horse
5. Put these black pieces on a horse's head
7. Female horse
8. Type of horse that looks hand painted
9. Popular horse race
10. Horse feed

ACROSS
3. Latin word for horse
6. Horses win these at racing competitions
7. Hair on the back of the neck
8. Another term for a "true bred" horse
10. You measure horses in "_____," not fingers

List your

Music Mania

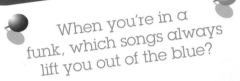

Music is a great way to cure boredom and get you in a groovy mood. Keep a record of your go-to tunes with these quick questions.

When you're in a funk, which songs always lift you out of the blue?

What are your top favorite guilty pleasure songs?

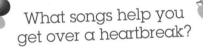
What songs help you get over a heartbreak?

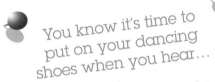
You know it's time to put on your dancing shoes when you hear…

What songs relate best to you when you're in a bad mood?

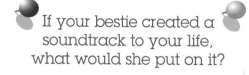
If your bestie created a soundtrack to your life, what would she put on it?

Beauty Parlor

Are you a super seeker? Put your eyes to the test and see if you can find 10 differences between the picture on the top and the one on the bottom.

Answer on page 270

FLOWER SHOP

Anchor
Biplane
Chess piece

Cow
Ice skates
Lion
Mouse

Snow blower
Tree ornament
Windmill

Recipes
DAIRY DREAMBOAT
Snacks

Dairy products are not only good tasting—they're good for you! Whip up some of this easy-to-make recipe to get closer to a healthier you.

INGREDIENTS & DIRECTIONS

You'll need:

- A small portion of cottage cheese

- Your favorite dried fruit (such as strawberry or blueberry)

- A small plastic container

Scoop the cottage cheese* into the container. Then mix in your choice of dried berries. Yum! What a quick and filling snack!

*Ask your parents if you have any allergies.

HAIRY SITUATION

Brush the hair out of your eyes. Can you find the two pictures that are exactly alike?

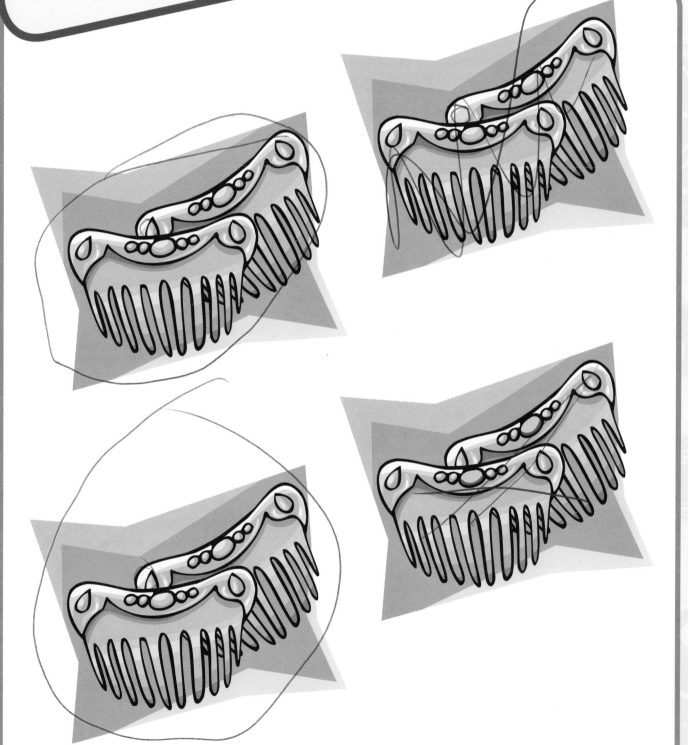

Color Me Happy!
Glamour TIPS

Highlight your natural beauty by using make-up colors that match your skin tone. What colors are best for you?

Peaches and Cream Complexion

Lips: Coral with a bit of glitter and some golden specks

Create a lipstick name that fits your personality: _____

Nails: Peaches, corals, toffees, and berries

Create a nail polish name that fits your personality: _____

Olive Complexion

Lips: Deep plums and roses

Create a lipstick name that fits your personality: _____

Nails: Pinky-beiges and corals

Create a nail polish name that fits your personality: _____

Pink and Fair Complexion

Lips: Pinks and roses

Create a lipstick name that fits your personality: _____

Nails: Pinks, ivories, and beiges

Create a nail polish name that fits your personality: _____

TRIP TO THE PET SHOP

Use the clues about cute pets to complete this crossword puzzle.

3 G O l d f i s h

6 t u s t l e

7 P u p p y

ACROSS
3 Orange-yellow aquarium dweller
5 Tiny, bright-colored parrot
6 Sometimes hides in its shell
7 Furry, with long ears

DOWN
1 Might run in a wheel
2 Small and scaly
4 Will grow up to chase mice
5 Baby version of "man's best friend"

What Does Your Room Say About You?

What if your walls could talk? Well, in a way, they do! Find out what your special space says about you by completing this fun quiz.

Free Spirit · Classic · Laid-Back

1. Which of the following best describes your favorite décor?
- a – A mish mash of styles, from wicker and wallpaper to hippie retro
- b – Everything color-coordinated, from bed sheets to curtains
- c – No real style, just simple and fun *A*

2. What kind of lighting do you prefer for your room?
- a – Lava lamps and candles *A*
- b – Nice, natural sunlight streaming through your windows
- c – Only as much as you need—an overhead light on the ceiling and a reading lamp by the bed

3. What kind of furniture do you like?
A
- a – It doesn't matter—you just paint everything silver, anyway
- b – A white canopy bed, with a matching nightstand and dresser
- c – The bare essentials—a comfortable bed, a few bookshelves, and a computer desk

4. Where do you do your homework?
A
- a – On the bed or at the dining-room table
- b – At the family's old writing desk
- c – At the computer desk

5. Which of the following best describes your wall art?
- a – Every inch is covered with rock star or day-glo posters, pictures of friends, and glow-in-the-dark stars
- b – Framed photos of friends and family are everywhere
- c – A calendar and a bulletin board pretty much mark the spot

Free Spirit

If you picked mostly "a" answers, you're a free spirit! Your room is a fun place, an excellent adventure where a lot is going on. You're a real individual who mixes up your décor and changes it according to how you feel.

Classic

If you picked mostly "b" answers, you're a classic chick! Your dream room is a calm, pleasant place where you can unwind and do your thing in a relaxed atmosphere. Having things match gives you a sense of order in your life.

Laid-Back

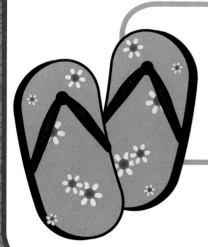

If you picked mostly "c" answers, you're a laid-back lady! You want a space that you can use and enjoy, not take care of all the time. As a result, your room is user-friendly and low-maintenance. You are a cool girl who isn't afraid to express her mellow mood.

WORDSMITH

Do you like writing? Maybe you're a wordsmith! Find these words that have to do with writing in the word search below. Look up, down, backward, forward, and diagonally.

Book	Fiction	Non-fiction	Novella	Poem
Essay	Memoir	Novel	Play	Short story

```
E P L H T P F R A E R S N R
I A Y L P O Y T T P E Y R E
B A F R O E Y A S S E D A E
B L R I O M E M L A V W N N
S L O D C T C D H P I G L I
R E I R I T S H I N M E S R
W V E T A C I T G S V K I W
E O C Q N E N O R O O T T H
E N O I T C I F N O N Y E I
N N U F T F Y O B M H A W B
A A S F O B P K H T Y S E F
J O S P N I E A L T A O F Y
T N C W C A Y N I B T U G A
D Q R P D Q T T M I F R R P
```

CUTE CUPCAKES

Fill in the blanks to complete this silly story about a tasty dessert. Pick a NOUN, ADJECTIVE, or VERB from the word bank to place in a corresponding blank, or think of your own weird words!

I love making cupcakes! The _Crunch_ [ADJECTIVE] part is _Spelling_ ing [VERB]

the finished cupcakes. There are lots of things you can _dump_ [VERB]

on a cupcake — _pizza_ [NOUN] usually goes on first. You can add

sprinkles, candy, or other sweet _Spider_ s. [NOUN] If it's someone's

good [ADJECTIVE] day, you can _dour_ [VERB] their name on the

cupcake. For birthdays, use a colorful _Bicycle_ [NOUN] in the middle.

See how _heavy_ [ADJECTIVE] you can make your next batch of cupcakes!

WORD BANK

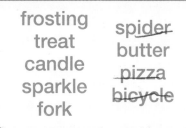

ADJECTIVES
best
special
pretty
toasty
gooey
crunchy
salty
slippery
heavy

NOUNS
frosting
treat
candle
sparkle
fork
spider
butter
pizza
bicycle

VERBS
color
dump
eat
dunk
play
toss
spell
roll
trick

Playground Paradise

Using the pictures below, complete this rebus puzzle about something you would find at a playground.

 - EY +  - CA + Y

+  - ABY +  - M

_ _ _ _ _ _

_ _ _ _

Answer on page 271

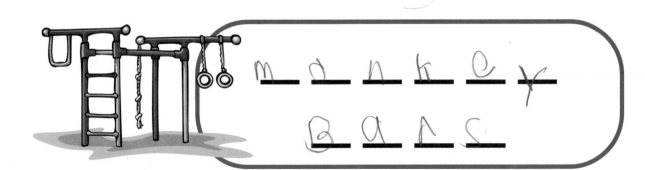

Let's Play House Maze

Follow the path from **Start** to **Finish** to get from the bottom of the tree to the tree house.

FINISH

START

Doodlin' >>>>>>>>>>>>>>>>>>>>>>>>>

School Dance Contest

Use your imagination to finish designing the prom dress and accessories for the school dance.

Write Your *Own Story*

When I grow up I want to be...

?

Recipes

BANANA-BERRY KABOBS
Snacks

Looking for a new way to eat healthy and still have fun? Serve these easy-to-make cool kabobs to your girlfriends for the perfect summertime sweet treat. Mix up the ingredients to include your favorite fruits!

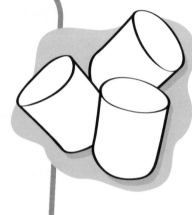

INGREDIENTS & DIRECTIONS

You'll need:

- 2 bananas
- 1 pint strawberries
- 1 cup mini marshmallows
- 4 kabob sticks

Peel the bananas* and carefully cut them into about 1" sections. Wash the berries and dry them with a paper towel. Slide the bananas, strawberries, and marshmallows onto the kabob sticks creating unique and colorful patterns. Enjoy!

*Ask your parents if you have any allergies.

Sudoku
FLAPPER GIRL

Put on your super chic thinking cap and try to decode this sudoku. Fill in the empty squares so that each row, column, and square contains the numbers 1–9 only once.

9	7	5	4	8	1	**3**	**6**	2
4	8	**6**	**5**	3	2	9	1	**7**
1	2	3	6	7	**9**	4	**5**	**8**
6	4	1	3	**2**	7	**5**		**9**
8	5	9	1	6	**4**	**2**	7	3
7	**3**	2	**9**	**5**	**8**	**6**	4	**1**
2	**9**	4	**7**	1	5	8	**3**	**6**
3	1	8	2	4	6	7	**9**	5
5	6	**7**	**8**	9	3	1	2	4

• List your Celebrity Crushes

Which celebrity crush makes you swoon—be it on the movie screen or TV screen, on stage, or somewhere in between? It's time to spill the beans on which hottie makes you blush.

 When it comes to Hollywood cuties, your leading men are...?

 Which TV megastars would you cast as your boyfriend?

 Guys who play in a band are always so good looking! Who are your top favorites?

 If you could bring to life five stud muffins from novels, who would they be?

  When it comes to celebrity crushes, your favorite facial features are...?

What's Your *Signature Scent?*

Follow this chart to figure out what kind of scent best fits your personality. At the end, you'll have a list of scents that just might be perfect for you!

Start

Do you prefer chocolate or vanilla?

Chocolate

Vanilla

Which seasons are your favorite?

Fall and Winter

Spring and Summer

New Years or Thanksgiving?

New Years

Thanksgiving

Do you prefer something sweet or something salty?

Sweet

Salty

What do you eat when you crave something sweet?

Candy

Fruit

What's your go-to seasonal pie?

Apple

Pumpkin

Do you like flowers?

Yes

No

FUN, SWEET SCENTS

Your love of sweets—from candies to fruits—makes you a natural fit for funky sweet scents like cotton candy, candy apple, raspberry, and cucumber melon.

WARM, COMFORTING SCENTS

You're a true comfort girl! You're at ease with warm, cozy scents like cinnamon, hot chocolate, vanilla sugar, and mistletoe.

CLEAN, FRESH, OR FLOWERY SCENTS

Use Mother Nature as your guide and seek out fresh natural scents like cotton, daffodil, wildflower, and springtime.

Lip Service
Glamour TIPS

Kiss dry, flaky lips goodbye! Say hello to a magnificent-looking mouth with a honey lip exfoliator. Pucker up!

LIP BALM

You'll need:

- Dab of honey
- Pinch of sugar

Combine the honey and sugar—just a few drops will work. Gently rub on moist lips. Rinse. Now your smacker is oh-so-sweet!

This lip exfoliator is great because it uses everyday ingredients.

SUPER SPACEY

Search, find, and circle these 10 things.

Bear
Crayons in box
Girl with pigtails

Girl with pink shirt
Horse
Ladybug
Mermaid

Palm trees
Princess hat
Witch

GLAMOUR GIRL

Change up your look with a little bit of glamour. Can you find the two pictures that are exactly alike?

Answer on page 272

Flower Power

Using the pictures below, complete this rebus puzzle about a type of flower.

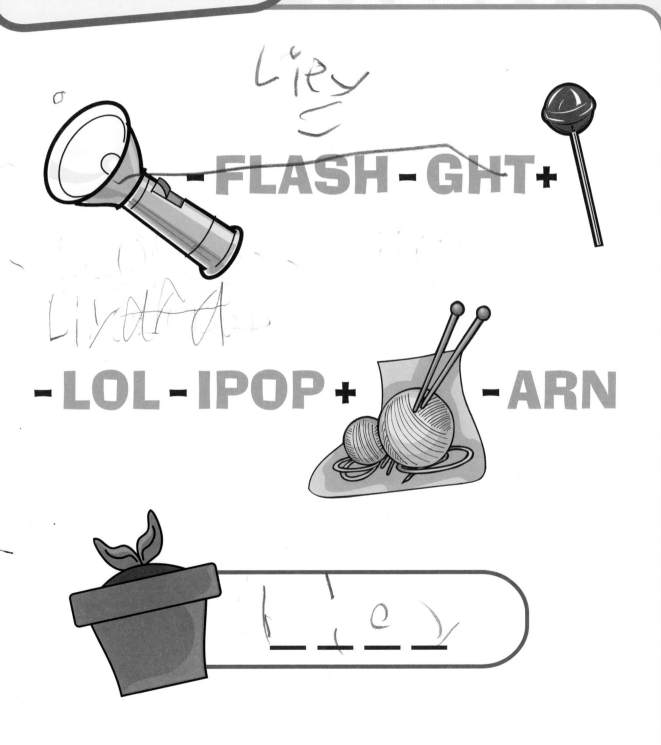

- FLASH - GHT +

- LOL - IPOP + - ARN

SOCCER GAME

Fill in the blanks to complete this silly story about a soccer game. Pick a NOUN, ADJECTIVE, or VERB from the word bank to place in a corresponding blank, or think of your own weird words!

It was the first soccer match of the season. The **feathery** [ADJECTIVE]

Flyers were facing the **gooey** [ADJECTIVE] Strikers. The first goal was

walk [VERB] ed after Jessie from the Flyers delivered a hard

muffin [NOUN]. The **kitten** [NOUN] went wild! The Strikers

climb [VERB] ed in a **book** [NOUN] at halftime. In the end, the Strikers

got a **pink** [ADJECTIVE] win and **dunk** [VERB] ed around the field!

WORD BANK

ADJECTIVES
ferocious
slow
talented
cute
surprising
funny
gooey
pink
feathery

NOUNS
kick
net
crowd
huddle
kitten
muffin
spoon
book
bicycle

VERBS
kick
talk
laugh
dunk
walk
bump
climb
deliver
gather

HigH HeeL MaNia

Are you a super seeker? Put your eyes to the test and see if you can find 10 differences between the picture on the top and the one on the bottom.

Answer on page 273

Let's Draw a
Giraffe Calf

On a separate piece of paper, follow these simple steps using a pencil and an eraser.

1 Start with a medium size oval for the main part of the body. Connect a half circle to create the hind end. Now, draw the long neck. Top it off with two ovals at the top of the neck, as shown.

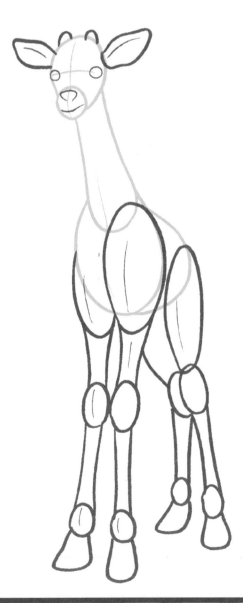

2 Giraffes have long legs with large knobby knees. Draw them as shown. Next, add the ears and sketch in the ears and some details on the face.

3 Now you can sketch more details. Add the tail and the spots. Erase any unwanted guidelines.

4 Once you add some color and shading, your giraffe will be ready to eat leaves off of tall trees.

Candy Shop Maze

Yum-yum, eat them up! Help this girl find her way to the candy shop by following the correct path through the maze. The correct path is made up of lollipops only.

START ↓

FINISH ↘

Candy Shop

54

• List your

Travelin' Woman

Whether you've been to all seven continents or stayed in the same town your whole life, now's the time to dream big about all the places you want to visit.

What country do you most want to visit? Why?

You can't leave home without...

What is the most favorite place you've visited?

If you were stuck on an island, which one would it be? Who would you be with?

When traveling, what is your favorite mode of transportation?

In the Bag
Glamour TIPS

No matter how many we have, it seems we can always use one more handbag. If you're looking for a new bag to hold your odds and ends check out these different styles.

What do you carry in your purse? _____
_____

What style best fits you? _____

Tote

This bag goes with just about any outfit. It's roomy and has inside pockets for your cell phone and wallet. Grab a tote and fill it with everything you need to get you through the day.

Cross-body Bag

If you are headed out and looking for something you won't have to worry about—try this bag. It fits snugly against your body and leaves you hands-free.

Clutch

This must-have little carry-along is perfect for special occasions. If you're headed to an event like a wedding, school dance, or fancy dinner, slip your lip gloss and keys into a clutch to dress up your outfit.

Rock and Roll

If you like to walk closer to fashion's wild side, try wearing a rocker-style purse. These bags are chock full of studs, zippers, and buckles —perfect for a night out with your friends!

Doodlin' Diving Divas

Use your imagination to finish designing the bathing suits for this swimwear collection.

How Do You Express Yourself?

Are you a natural leader or more of a go-with-the-flow kind of girl? Take this quiz and find out.

Follower · In Between · Leader

1. **Teacher's conference day is coming up and you're psyched for the day off from school. You're most likely to—**
   a - Scan the newspaper's events section the week before and plan an entire, fun-filled day for you and your friends. (2)
   b - Wait for one of your friends to call you with an idea on how to spend the day. (1)

2. **Your favorite band is coming to the local arena and you think it might be cool to get all your friends together for a party before the concert. You're most likely to—**
   a - Avoid the hassle and just go to the show with a friend or two. Planning a party is too much work! (1)
   b - Dive into the plans headfirst, and make it the most awesome pre-concert bash ever! (2)

3. **Your parents' 20th anniversary is coming up and you would love to throw them a big surprise party. You're most likely to—**
   a - Suggest it to your older siblings, or aunts and uncles, and offer your help in any way possible. (1)
   b - Come up with a plan for the big bash, then take it to your siblings. (2)

4. **You've just learned that a new dress-code rule has been issued at school. You think the rule is totally unfair. You're most likely to—**
   a - Get a group of kids together and start a petition. (2)
   b - Sign any anti-dress code petition that is passed in front of you. (1)

5. **Over the next three Saturday nights, you're most likely to—**
   a - Wait for your buds to let you know what's up. (1)
   b - Call for movie time, then pick a flick for you and your buds to see. (2)

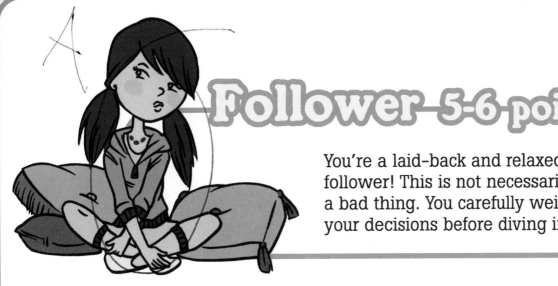

Follower 5-6 points

You're a laid-back and relaxed follower! This is not necessarily a bad thing. You carefully weigh your decisions before diving in.

In Between 7-8 points

You're a "when the mood strikes" kind of leader! You enjoy taking charge once in a while, and though you may be hesitant to go the distance to take charge, you don't like to sit back and go with the flow.

Leader 9-10 points

You're a natural-born leader! You are comfortable with who you are and have no problem looking, thinking, and acting the way you like. You are a trailblazer!

How To TIPS
Redo Your Room

Has your bedroom looked the same for years? Learn how to make your room go from somber to stylin' with these tips.

DOOR DÉCOR

Is the door to your room exciting? Choose a décor that represents who you are. If there's something or someone you're totally into (think a swoon-worthy celebrity!), hang pictures, posters, or prints on the outside of your door.

HOW'S IT HANGING?

It's time to give your wall a wake-up call with some new treatments. If you're into the latest styles, you can create a decoupage wall hanging from your favorite fashion magazines.

SPORTS NUT

If you're a huge sports fan, use pictures from sports magazines to make a custom screen of your favorite sports star. Stick the print pages to a posterboard with tape.

CUSTOM COMFORT

Custom is the hot word in the decorating world. Maybe what you need is a little splash of paint! Ask your parents for permission before you do anything major.

Sudoku
PLAYING DRESS UP

Put on a silly outfit and try to decode this sudoku. Fill in the empty squares so that each row, column, and square contains the numbers 1–9 only once.

	5			7				
8	3		6		4		7	
2				3			5	
						8	2	3
	4				6	7		
3		7						6
	6			1				
5	8		2	4	3			
7	9		5		8			2

SECRET CRUSH

Fill in the blanks to complete this silly story about a secret crush. Pick a NOUN, ADJECTIVE, or VERB from the word bank to place in a corresponding blank, or think of your own weird words!

I sometimes see my secret crush at _____ [NOUN] and usually I want to run and _____ [VERB]! When I see my crush, my cheeks turn _____ [ADJECTIVE] and I feel _____ [ADJECTIVE]. Sometimes my _____ [NOUN]s tease me! Only a few _____ [ADJECTIVE] people know about my crush. We like to _____ [VERB] about our crushes at _____ [NOUN]. It's fun to _____ [VERB] about a secret crush!

WORD BANK

ADJECTIVES
gross
~~red~~
golden
dizzy
unlucky
sticky
special
~~bold~~
~~angry~~

NOUNS
class
school
homework
~~friend~~
~~cookie~~
sleepover
puppy
~~circus~~
gym

VERBS
hide
talk
giggle
swim
~~slip~~
grin
dance
~~trick~~
stare

WORK OF ART

Think you're a real Picasso? Then you'll enjoy this activity! Find these types of works of art in the word search below. Look up, down, backward, forward, and diagonally.

Carving	Drawing	Modern art	Painting	Sculpture
Ceramics	Exhibit	Mural	Portrait	Watercolor

```
E B I U N R Y K W E Y W E A
Y C F H P C K T T T O R G V
E A C C D E A C F F U J T A
W R E P R R L X G T E P R T
O V O X V A K G P H T O T G
D I P L H M N L A L B R O Q
G N E F O I U O S D A T H S
L G Z M T C B N N N R R E B
E K E N S S R I R Z D A U F
M S I D O P D E T B A I E M
K A T R A Z D I T G V T N M
P O N U E O K Q L A I B P A
K L E G M D G G N I W A R D
R G O F H N E Y H L E T A L
```

AMAZING ANIMALS

Use the clues about amazing animals to complete this crossword puzzle.

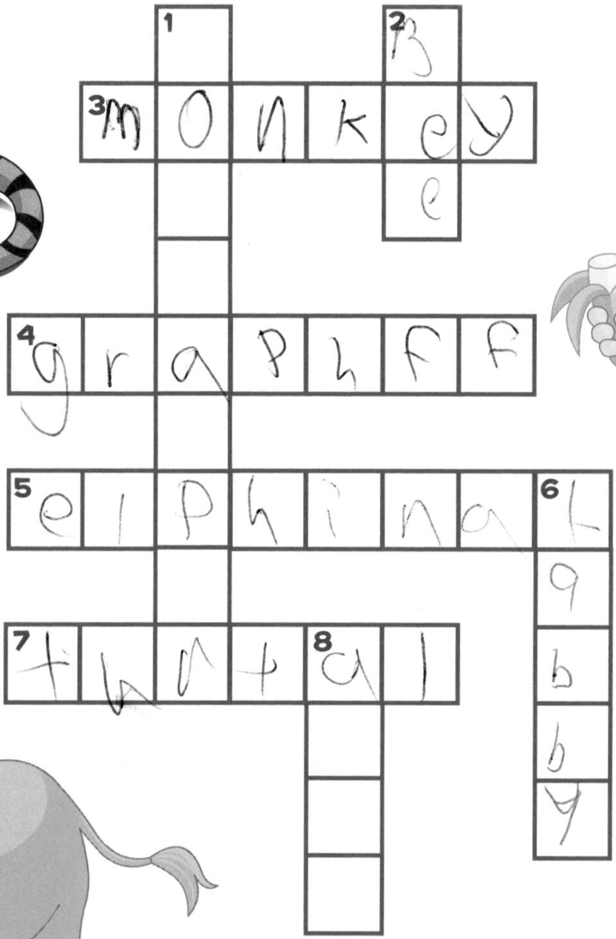

ACROSS
3 Swings in a tree
4 Long neck
5 Big trunk
7 Slow moving, loves water

DOWN
1 White and furry
2 Lives in a hive
6 Striped cat
8 Big mane

Answer on page 274

Doodlin' Wedding Bliss

>>>>>>>>>>>>>>>>>>>>>>>>

Use your imagination to finish designing the wedding dress and accessories for this bride.

How To TIPS

Do you like to watch little kids? Do you think of yourself as a little "mother's helper"? If so, you and your friends might be good babysitters! Follow these babysitting guidelines to help you create a babysitting club.

Start a Babysitting Club

THE LIST

Before you can start babysitting, you need to develop a client list. Some places to consider for families are at friends' houses, neighborhood meetings, and school.

CREATE FLIERS

Another way to get a babysitting job is to advertise. You and your friends can create fliers with your expertise. Have you watched kids before? Do you know CPR? These are all good things to list.

Babysitter

call me

BABY BASICS

Ask your parents for help with babysitting skills. Have them explain things like how to feed a baby, how to change a diaper, what to do in case of an emergency, and how much to charge, if any. See if you can take a CPR class, too!

WHAT NOT TO WEAR

Be sure to wear babysitting appropriate clothes. That means no long earrings and no dressy clothes. Sometime babysitting is dirty work!

SOMETHING'S COOKIN'

Are you a super seeker? Put your eyes to the test and see if you can find 10 differences between the picture on the top and the one on the bottom.

Answer on page 274

Recipes

SWEET & SALTY PARTY MIX
Snacks

This simple party mix is the perfect combination of sweet and salty—so everyone will be happy! Whip it up the next time you're having friends over for a get-together.

INGREDIENTS & DIRECTIONS

You'll need:

- 1 box cheddar cheese crackers
- 1 bag mini pretzels
- 1 bag candy-coated chocolate pieces

Mix all of the ingredients* together. Pour the party mix into a big bowl and serve! (Store the extra mix in a tightly covered container, so it will stay fresh for your next party.)

*Ask your parents if you have any allergies.

List your
Lottery Wish List

Congrats! You've just won the lottery. You're now a millionaire! Make some lists of what you will do next.

What are your winning numbers? Are they special?

What are the first three things you will buy?

What is the biggest thing you plan on buying?

You can now make your own invention. It can be whatever you like! What is it?

Who do you plan on sharing your newfound wealth with?

Perfect Skin Strategies
Glamour TIPS

Skin comes in lots of different types, but all skin is sensitive and needs some attention! Check out these skin care tips and you'll have a healthy glow in no time.

DON'T OVERDO IT!

There are lots of creams and washes designed to give you healthy skin, but using too many or too much can give you the opposite effect. Try sticking to one or two that work for you, and use them only as often as the directions say.

WONDERFUL WATER

Everyone knows that drinking plenty of water is part of staying healthy, but did you know it can also keep your skin clear and shine free? Drinking eight or more glasses of water a day will not only make you feel great, you'll look great, too!

SUNNY SKIN

It's always a good idea to wear sunscreen, especially if you have a fair complexion. Applying sunscreen to your face is a smart move if you want perfect skin—bad sunburns can lead to skin problems and even wrinkles when you're older!

HANDS OFF!

When you're in class do you rest your chin on your palm? Lots of us do—but our skin's natural oils can become trapped in our pores this way. The result may be pimples, so be sure to keep your hands off!

Getting perfect skin takes commitment and consistency! Use the space below to record what you've done for your skin each day of the week, whether it's how many glasses of water you've had, or if you've gone the whole day without resting your head on your hand.

SUNDAY _____
MONDAY _____
TUESDAY _____
WEDNESDAY _____
THURSDAY _____
FRIDAY _____
SATURDAY _____

SUNDAY _____
MONDAY _____
TUESDAY _____
WEDNESDAY _____
THURSDAY _____
FRIDAY _____
SATURDAY _____

SUNDAY _____
MONDAY _____
TUESDAY _____
WEDNESDAY _____
THURSDAY _____
FRIDAY _____
SATURDAY _____

SUNDAY _____
MONDAY _____
TUESDAY _____
WEDNESDAY _____
THURSDAY _____
FRIDAY _____
SATURDAY _____

MOVIE MARATHON

Fill in the blanks to complete this silly story about watching movies. Pick a NOUN, ADJECTIVE, or VERB from the word bank to place in a corresponding blank, or think of your own weird words!

The most important part of a movie marathon is the ___rocket ship___
[NOUN]

Once that's all set, make sure everyone is ___shiny___ and ready
[ADJECTIVE]

to ___tickle___ some movies! It's ___silky___ to have a balance
[VERB]   [ADJECTIVE]

of movie types, because not everyone ___juggle___s the same
[VERB]

thing. ___comfy___ movies make some people ___sleep___, and
[ADJECTIVE]   [VERB]

___ghost___ movies can scare some people! Before you ___squirm___
[NOUN]   [VERB]

another movie, take a ___bubblegum___ break. Some people might
[NOUN]

___gulp___ or get ___expensive___, but the marathon goes on!
[VERB]   [ADJECTIVE]

WORD BANK

ADJECTIVES	NOUNS	VERBS
comfy, long, smart, shiny, romantic, silly, scary, expensive, bored	mystery, snack, popcorn, cowboy, action, rocket ship, bubblegum, comedy, ghost	watch, juggle, blink, gulp, like, squirm, start, tickle, sleep

FIERCE MANICURE

Bright nail designs demand attention. Can you find the two pictures that are exactly alike?

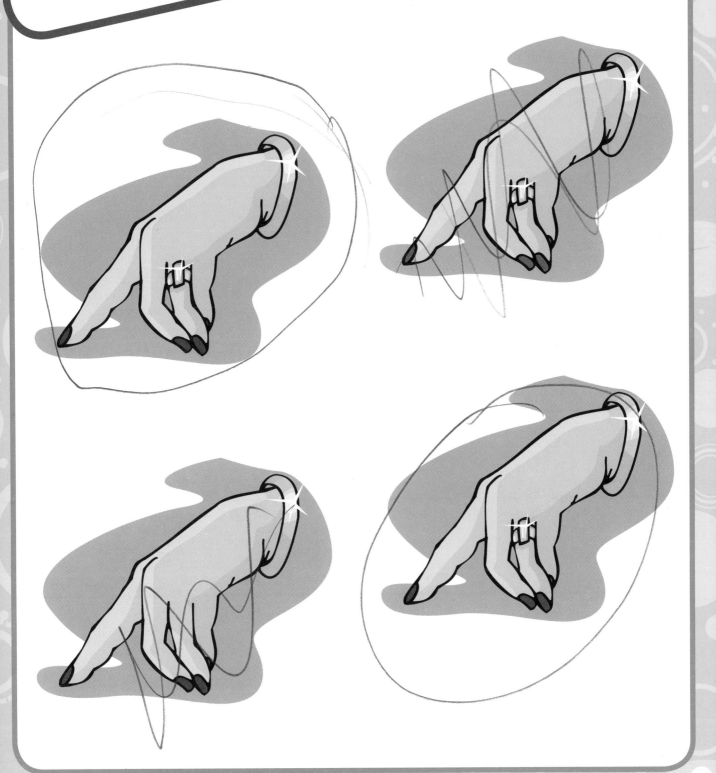

Answer on page 274

Sudoku
TEA-TIME

Grab a cup of tea and try to decode this sudoku. Fill in the empty squares so that each row, column, and square contains the numbers 1–9 only once.

			4	3			8	
4	3			7	5			
		2				7		
8				1		9		
	6		9		7	4	3	
3		9						
6	9	7	5					
	8						5	
	2			8	6		7	

Answer on page 274

CITY LIVING

Search, find, and circle these 10 things.

Dog   Kayak   Teddy bear
Horse   Pink tutu   Turtle
Jump rope   Pretzel   Washing machine
Red purse

Answer on page 275

Are You an Introvert or an Extrovert?

Read each statement, and then put a check under "Like Me" or "Not Like Me." When you're done, go to the end of the quiz to find out your personality type!

LIKE ME   NOT LIKE ME

1. I wear lots of bright colors.

2. I prefer calling my friends instead of texting them.

3. I like doing homework in a quiet place, like the library.

4. I usually hang out with small groups of people.

5. When my friends and I go to the movies, I usually pick what we see.

6. In school, I prefer working individually instead of in groups.

7. I always raise my hand before saying something in class.

8. If I have a crush, I tell everyone I know about it!

9. My friends are always asking me for advice.

10. I would rather be treasurer than class president.

11. I always ask for solos in music class.

12. Sometimes I get in trouble for talking during study hall.

13. I've always had more best friends than acquaintances.

14. I get very nervous before giving a presentation in class.

15. I like to make my plans for the weekend early in the week.

Tally it up!

If you chose mostly "Like Me" you're not afraid to speak your mind and get involved with social events. Some people even call you a "Social Butterfly"!

If you chose mostly "Not Like Me" answers, you are an introvert! You tend to get the most fun out of doing low-key events with a small group of people instead of a crowd. You make and maintain strong relationships with your close group of friends.

TRIP TO THE MALL

Time to go to the mall! Can you find the two pictures that are exactly alike?

Answer on page 275

List your
Dream School

You spend a lot of time in school. What if you could make a few changes to make it all your own? Have fun filling in the following school-time daydreams!

 If you could design the school's lunch program, what would be on the menu?

 Would you have a school uniform?

 What celebrities would you hire as teachers?

 What would the school mascot be?

 What classes would you like taught in school?

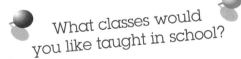

79

How To TIPS
Double-Dutch

Double dutch is a lot like jump rope—except it's even cooler because you use two ropes! Grab two of your friends and get ready for the three of you to have some fun. Use these tips for some guidance.

PRETTY BASIC

To play, you need to have at least three people and two extra-long jump ropes. Two people will be in charge of swinging the rope up and down, with the left hand clockwise and the right one counterclockwise. The other person, the jumper, will be jumping the rope.

FINDING THE RHYTHM

Like jump rope, the jumper will need to jump over the rope, not on it. She has to worry about two ropes now though! Once the jumper has developed a rhythm, more jumpers can hop in and join the game.

SING A SONG

Since multiple people can play double dutch at a time, you can have more fun than you do just jumping rope alone. Try singing songs together. There are already some popular double-dutch songs.

Here are a few double-dutch songs:

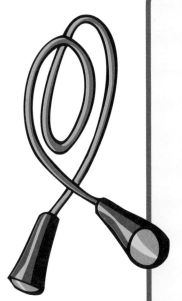

Miss Mary Mack, Mack, Mack ,
All dressed in black, black, black,
With silver buttons, buttons, buttons,
All down her back, back, back.

She asked her mother, mother, mother,
For fifteen cents, cents, cents,
To see the elephant, elephant, elephant,
Jump the fence, fence, fence.

He jumped so high, high, high.
He reached the sky, sky, sky.
And he never came back, back, back,
Till the Fourth of July, lie, lie.

Cinderella, dressed in yellow,
Went upstairs to kiss a fellow,
Made a mistake,
Kissed a snake,
How many doctors
Did it take?
1, 2, 3...
(count until someone makes a mistake)

Bubblegum, bubblegum, in a dish,
How many pieces do you wish?
1, 2, 3...
(count until someone makes a mistake)

PENGUIN MAZE

Follow the path from **Start** to **Finish** to help the penguins get to the water.

START

FINISH

Answer on page 275

Are you a super seeker? Put your eyes to the test and see if you can find 10 differences between the picture on the left and the one on the right.

Answer on page 275

MUSIC LOVER

Whether it's from your headphones or from a speaker, you like to rock out to music. Find these types of music styles in the word search below. Look up, down, backward, forward, and diagonally.

Alternative	**Dance**	**House**	**Pop**	**Reggae**
Classical	**Hip hop**	**Opera**	**Rap**	**Rock**

```
K O F R K P A W S A E N M S
H L S R C C H O I C V L N M
N Z O E N O J Z N J I S T I
Y Q A P Z L E A N W T D M M
S S E N E C D D J J A O Y E
J R B S Q R O Z V G N U I P
F A A E U E A G G E R I A N
S C P F R O Q Q M O E R H L
P G P S E H H Q X V T O C S
B W C L A C I S S A L C Y E
E Q P E S S P V E R A K E A
E C T V C X H P R O T C E O
J I E O G I O O R C P J H S
C O S D Y P P M Z X E J G M
```

Answer on page 276

Sudoku
SOMBRERO

You'll have a real party trying to decode this sudoku. Fill in the empty squares so that each row, column, and square contains the numbers 1–9 only once.

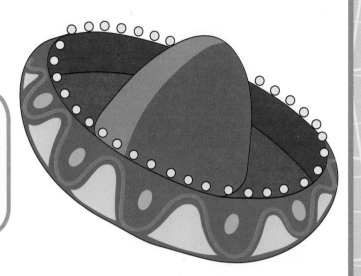

		2	4	8	7	3	6	
			1	5	2		7	
		8		3				
			9	6				8
				4				
6	4		3		8	9		
			8		3		5	
2	3					4		
7				9			3	6

Answer on page 276

Abracadabra!

Using the pictures below, complete this rebus puzzle about small and sparkly creatures.

- AZ - NE + 🕯 - ND - E

magical

F + 🚪 - H + 👔 - T + S

Fairies

___m___a___g___c___a___l___
___f___a___i___r___i___e___r___

Answer on page 276

Where's Your
Spring Break
Destination?

Follow this chart to figure out the perfect spot to spend your spring break. At the end, you'll find the destination that just might be perfect for you!

Start

During your free time you prefer to:

Relax

Be on the go

You enjoy visiting:

Miles of sandy beaches

Historical sites

Natural beauty

At outdoor concerts, you like to listen to:

Pop

Reggae

Rock

Given the option, you would rather eat:

Fresh fruit

Hot dogs

You would rather unwind with:

A magazine   A facial

TANNING ON THE BEACH
Your love for fresh fruit and reading magazines show that you like to relax. All arrows point to sunny beaches for your ideal Spring Break destination!

CAMPING IN THE MOUNTAINS
You're a girl on the go! Hiking, hot dogs, and a love for natural beauty perfectly describe a camping hot spot!

BIG CITY SITES
You love being active and checking out historical sites—book your ticket now to a big city... get tickets to a rock concert while you're at it!

Write Your
Own Story

Get inspired and write your own story about if you were a rock star.

If I was a rock star...

COOL GIRL

What does it take to be a cool girl? Find some of characteristics of a cool girl in the word search below. Look up, down, backward, forward, and diagonally.

Athletic	Fashion	Fun	Hobbies	Smart
Confidence	Friends	Happy	Nice	Smile

```
I L S D O Z Q R K E O S I C
E L O S N Y F T E L I M S Y
Z E C N E D I F N O C A R K
K O W I W H S D N E I R F B
U L Z Q S N E L E H T T N H
Z R S I R W O Y I P E N O R
R P R E A E C I N E L U S Y
P E S E I B B O H R H F P U
X M I X O F R U J S T P V P
E R C K E E J W D D A C C S
I D Y M E O O O Q H Q F P S
Z F E O M C S H H Y V H D O
E C O M D S H G T N I J F N
U V D M R A B E C R N V N E
```

Answer on page 276

COLOR MANIA

Use the clues about colors to complete this crossword puzzle.

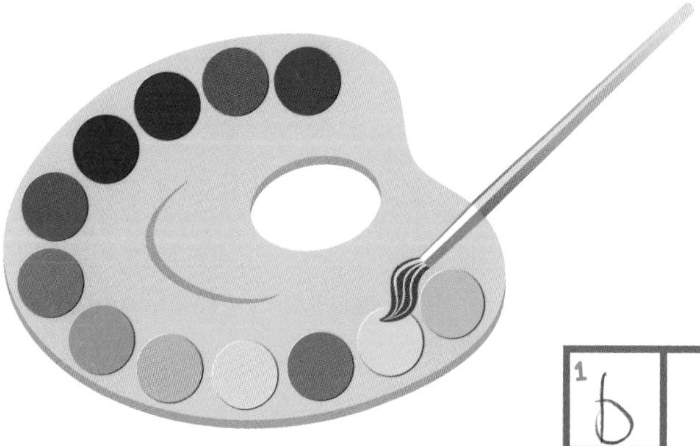

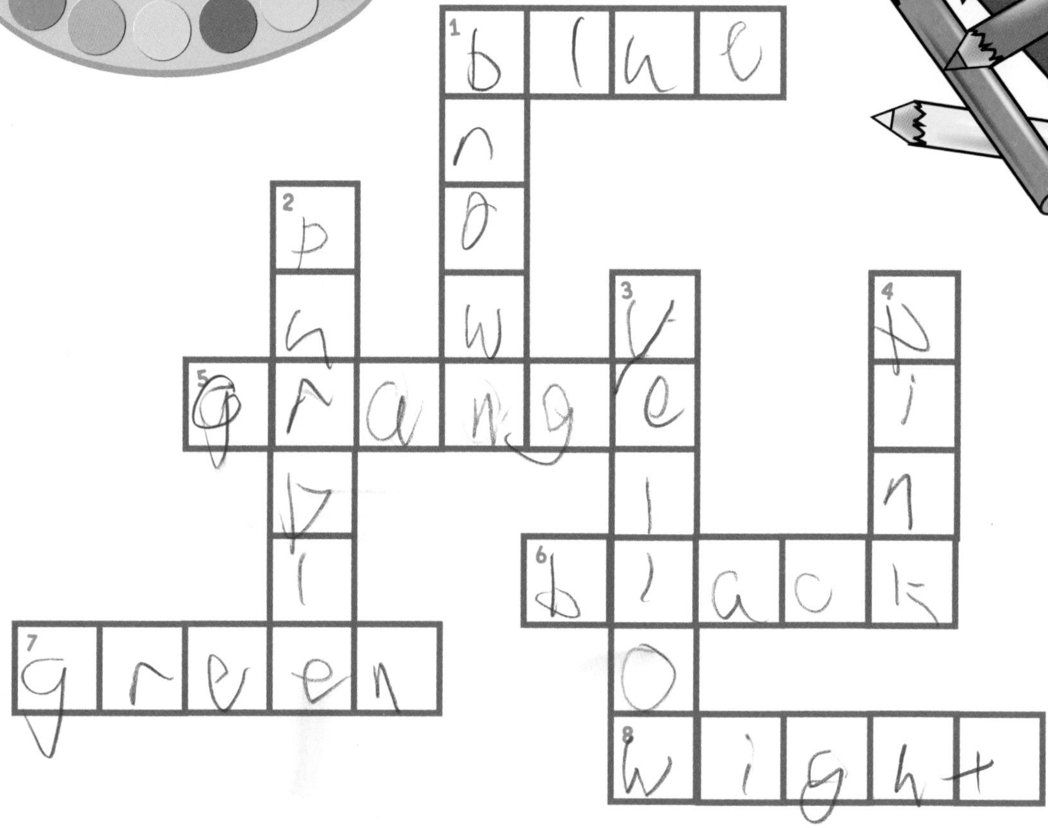

ACROSS

1. Color of the sky
5. Red + yellow = ___________
6. All the colors mixed together make this
7. Color of the grass
8. Color of the clouds

DOWN

1. Color of chocolate
2. Red + blue = ___________
3. Color of the sun
4. Shade of red

Answer on page 277

LET'S SHOP

Fill in the blanks to complete this silly story about shopping. Pick a NOUN, ADJECTIVE, or VERB from the word bank to place in a corresponding blank, or think of your own weird words!

The _____ is full of _____ and interesting
　　　　[NOUN]　　　　　　　　　　[ADJECTIVE]

stores. If you _____ something in a window, go
　　　　　　　[VERB]

inside and check it out! Part of the fun is _____ing
　　　　　　　　　　　　　　　　　　　　　　[VERB]

for the best _____. Mix and match _____
　　　　　　　　[NOUN]　　　　　　　　　　　　[ADJECTIVE]

colors to create a _____ style. Find a special
　　　　　　　　　　　[ADJECTIVE]

_____ to complete your look. The hardest part
　　[NOUN]

about shopping is trying to _____ all your bags!
　　　　　　　　　　　　　　　　[VERB]

WORD BANK

ADJECTIVES	NOUNS	VERBS
cool royal smart different tricky unique boring chilly ancient	mall snake bow tie accessory pretzel bargain balloon pony sandwich	crawl draw see search carry throw find talk look

Recipes

CRAZY CRACKER STACKERS

Snacks

Put a new spin on boring sandwiches with a crazy cracker stacker. Make this finger food for a fun lunch or a quick and tasty snack.

INGREDIENTS & DIRECTIONS

You'll need:

- 12 crackers
- An assortment of deli meats like turkey, ham, and salami
- **Slices of your favorite cheese**
- Optional: mustard, peanut butter, jelly, pickle chips… anything you like on your sandwich!

Build your stacker* high or keep it short—use your creativity! Invite your friends over to find out how they build their cracker stacker. The possibilities are endless!

*Ask your parents if you have any allergies.

CHICK FLICK

Cat
Fairy
Horse

Pie
Purple hair bow
Purple purse
Snow globe

Strawberry
Violin
Watermelon

Birthday Party Maze

Happy birthday! Help this girl get to her friend's birthday party by following the correct path through the maze. The correct path is made up of party hats only.

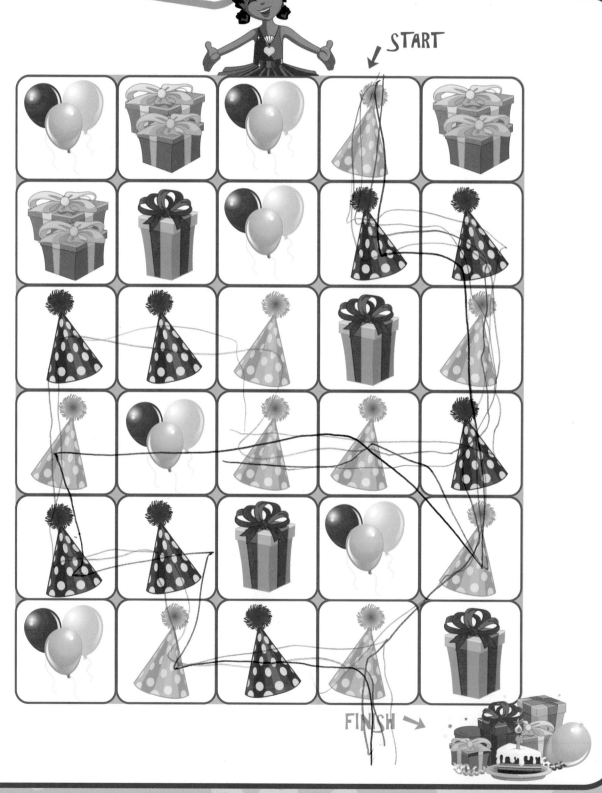

START

FINISH →

Answer on page 277

Doodlin' >>>>>>>>>>>>>>>>>>>>>>>>>>
Cha-Cha-Chica

Use your imagination and draw the perfect partner for this flamenco dancer.

So Many Shoes
Glamour
TIPS

Here is a foot-friendly guide to all types of different shoes. With the perfect pair, you'll be going places!

High Heels

- Stilettos have sky-high, thin heels and are worn at fancy events.

- Kitten heels are short and pointy—more ideal for everyday.

- Peep toes have an opening at the tip of the toes and are fun to wear to parties.

Sandals

- Flat sandals are open in the front and the back—great for everyday wear in warm weather.

- Flip flops are completely open except for a strap that you slip your foot into and are perfect for the beach.

Flats

- Ballerina flats are exactly how they sound—they resemble a dancer shoe and are super comfy. A great choice for school.

- Slingbacks have a closed toe and open heel. A strap around the heel keeps the shoe in place—dress them up or dress them down.

LOVE SONG

Make the apple of your eye sing with a sweet melody. Can you find the two pictures that are exactly alike?

Answer on page 277

PUPPIES GALORE

Woof woof! Puppies are so cute! Find these types of puppies in the word search below. Look up, down, backward, forward, and diagonally.

Bulldog	Papillon	Poodle	Puli	Spaniel
Husky	Pointer	Pug	Shih Tzu	Terrier

```
A A A T G O T R N T B J J D
H O P D O I E N E F N J S A
L N M L S F E S V E G N N I
R A S E P W Z A Z S O O D I
V T H X C K N N S L D Q R A
H O I X N R M O L T L J H G
B T H N K G P I D H L O E J
R E T N I O P H I L U P L F
T R Z S P A N I E L B S L E
T R U E P O O D L E Q S K M
A I C C J D E G K F C A P Y
S E G U Q F N V U C M H V P
R R E N M M N E O P E F M Y
B M M H T U R S E S R T U I
```

Answer on page 278

• List your Summer Souvenirs

Remember your carefree summer by completing these fun questions. You'll be able to keep your summer highlights for years to come—way longer than the ones in your hair!

 Where did you spend your summer?

 What did you do when the weather was bad?

 What is your most favorite memory of the summer?

 Who helped make this the best summer ever?

 What was the last thing you did before starting school?

How Do You Act Around Your Secret Crush?

Does your secret crush know that you like them? Take this quiz to find out if you're keeping a good secret, or if the cat's out of the bag!

Secretive · Mysterious · Flirt

1. Your crush walks by your locker. You:
a - Continue gathering up your books and don't look in their direction. (1)
b - Smile at them, worrying that your cheeks are turning red. (2)
c - Try to climb into your locker and hide. (3)

2. How well do you know your crush's friends?
a - You have some classes with them and make an effort to chat when you can. (2)
b - Very well! They've told you about the kind of music your crush likes, what clubs they belong to, what they do after school. (3)
c - You avoid them. What if your crush saw you talking to them and came over to say "Hi"? (1)

3. You got the lead role in the school play, and your crush was picked as the other lead! What do you do?
a - Panic and offer your role up to someone else who wants it. There are plenty of smaller roles left anyway. (2)
b - Keep your cool and remember to really nail your lines for the next rehearsal. (1)
c - Get a little nervous, but maybe this means you can spend some time practicing lines with your crush. (1)

4. Your crush has a big lacrosse match coming up. Some of your friends are planning to go, do you join them?
a - Yes, I never miss a chance to do something fun with my friends. (1)
b - Yeah, that could be fun! I'll wear the team's colors, paint my crush's number on my cheek, and write a cute cheer! (3)
c - Sure, maybe if my crush scores I can congratulate them in class the next day. (2)

5. You're planning your birthday party. Do you invite your crush?
a - Invite my crush? Are you crazy? Well, maybe I could hand him an invitation…why are my hands so sweaty? (3)
b - I would send my crush an invitation in the mail, but I'd be sure to ask them for the right address first. (2)
c - I'm sure my crush will hear about the party from other people at school. (1)

Secretive 5-6 points

Your secret crush is clueless! Try opening up a little around him. Throw a compliment to him now and again, and with time, he'll know you're into him.

Mysterious 7-8 points

Your secret crush might know you're crushing! Sometimes you're direct and sometimes you're not. Your poor crush doesn't know what to think! Consider making the next move and making your interest better known.

Flirt 9-10 points

Your secret crush definitely knows! You're direct with your flirting—there's no way he couldn't know. You should just come clean and see if he feels the same. The two of you could be a dynamic duo!

FRIENDS FOREVER

Fill in the blanks to complete this silly story about best friends. Pick a NOUN, ADJECTIVE, or VERB from the word bank to place in a corresponding blank, or think of your own weird words!

A friend is a _Ugly_ person who will always be there for you.
[ADJECTIVE]

Lots of people make or do things for their _Friend_s, like making
[NOUN]

_Bumblebee_s or _lungy_ing to _depraibu_ places together.
[NOUN]   [VERB]   [ADJECTIVE]

Friends may have just met, or have known each other for a long

kite. If friends _go_ away from each other, they
[NOUN]   [VERB]

usually stay in touch. Friends know each other's _Special_
[ADJECTIVE]

secrets, even if they're embarrassing! Who's your Forever Friend?

Call or write them, just to say "Hello!"
[VERB]

WORD BANK

ADJECTIVES	NOUNS	VERBS
unruly	friend	go
dependable	kite	speak
special	macaroni	whisper
warm	bracelet	move
colorful	time	call
ugly	dessert	crawl
curly	bumble bee	throw
boring	pet	dig
sweet	hat	lunge

FLOWER FUN

Are you a super seeker? Put your eyes to the test and see if you can find 10 differences between the picture on the left and the one on the right.

Answer on page 278

Write Your
Own Story

My best kept secret is... **?**

TOP SECRET

How To TIPS

In the summertime when the weather is hot, there's nothing more refreshing than a tall glass of lemonade and some cookies! Learn how to set up your lemonade and cookies stand with these quick tips.

Lemonade & Cookies Stand

THE ESSSENTIALS

Grab a friend or two and build an outline of a stand. The basic items you will need are two chairs for you to sit in, a short table to put your supplies on, and your homemade goodies.

LOOKIE HERE!

To draw more attention to your stand, you and your friends should make signs to hang on the table. Write things like "Best Lemonade Ever!" and "Homemade Cookies—Made from Scratch!"

TIP YOUR HAT

After working hard from setting up your stand and making your food, you deserve to get some kind of reward. Create a cute tip jar for your stand from a pickle jar and decorate it with stickers.

Heavenly Scents
Glamour TIPS

Did you know that certain scents make you feel a certain way? Aromatherapy uses scents to change your mood. Use the guidelines to learn more about aromatherapy.

Citrus

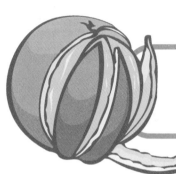

Sniffing the peels of oranges, lemons, limes, and grapefruits will give you an uplifting, invigorating boost. Try this in the morning when you need a little help getting up and on the go!

Floral

Flowery scents help with relaxation. Sit a pretty bouquet on your bedside table and inhale the scents for a good night's sleep.

Vanilla

Taking a whiff of this sweet scent will help you quickly calm down. So, if a visit to the dentist's office jangles your nerves, dab some vanilla on a tissue and bring it with you!

What is your favorite scent? _____

What does it say about you?_____

_____

GIRL TALK

Girls just love to talk! Can you find the two pictures that are exactly alike?

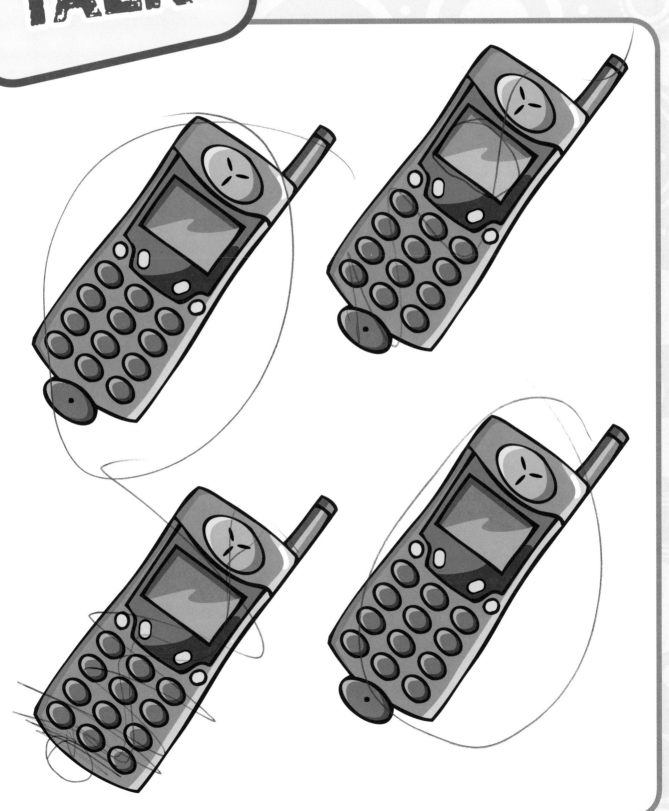

Answer on page 278

Let's Draw a
Chick

On a separate piece of paper, follow these simple steps using a pencil and an eraser.

1 Baby chicks can be drawn by using only a few simple shapes. Start with a large oval for the body, as shown. Then, draw the head shape with a simple beak.

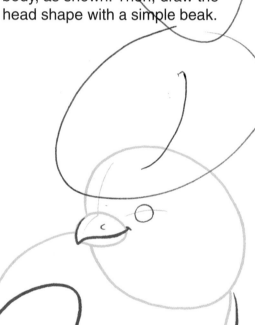

2 Next, add the wing shape. Sketch in the two legs, as shown. Lightly sketch in the eye shape and start to define the beak.

3 Now is the fun part. Add some fluff to the chicks body and finish off the leg details.

4 Add some color or shading to complete. This little chick is ready to explore the farm!

How Do You Get Your Exercise?

Cardio · Weights · Sports

1. How would you describe your study routine?
- a – I like to bring my notes to a study group—I work best with other people. (3)
- b – Slow and steady. I don't mind taking a while to get something right. (2)
- c – Alone, with music playing. Sometimes being a little distracted helps. (3)

2. It's time to relax! What are your plans?
- a – Spend some time trying to beat my friend's high score in our favorite video game! (2)
- b – Take a load off and read something I've been meaning to get to. (1)
- c – Round up all my friends and head out for a night at the movies. (3)

3. It's time to pick a sport in gym class. What do you pick?
- a – Soccer, volleyball, lacrosse, kickball…I can't make a decision! (3)
- b – Step aerobics or pilates—something that I can do while zoning out. (1)
- c – Volleyball, baseball, or anything that doesn't involve too much moving around! (2)

4. What type of movie do you like the best?
- a – Action movies (2)
- b – Sports movies (3)
- c – Spy movies (1)

5. How do you feel about "alone time?"
- a – I don't mind it all. (1)
- b – It's OK, everyone needs some now and then. (2)
- c – I hate it! (3)

Cardio 5-8 points

You like cardio! Things like running, jogging, walking, and using machines like treadmills are all great for your heart. You may prefer to work out alone, and might even benefit from the quiet time alone.

Weights 9-11 points

You like lifting weights! You don't mind working out around people, but being alone isn't a problem, either. You are focused on overcoming sizable goals!

Sports 12-15 points

You like team sports! You do your best when surrounded by others to push and support you. You're naturally competitive, so use this to your advantage while maintaining a healthy regimen.

Dude Ranch Maze

Follow the path from **Start** to **Finish** to help the cowgirl get through the cactus patch.

Answer on page 278

Sudoku
BASEBALL FUN

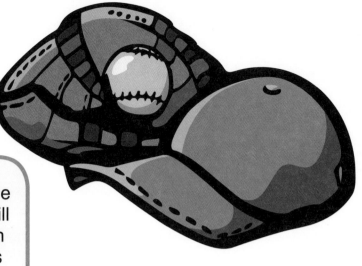

Use your math skills on and off the field. Try to decode this sudoku. Fill in the empty squares so that each row, column, and square contains the numbers 1–9 only once.

		7			2		4	6
			7	4				3
			6			2		5
5						3		
	4		3				6	8
3	7		2	8		4	9	
	6	9				8		
				5		7		4
		4			7	6		

Fashion Do's and Don'ts

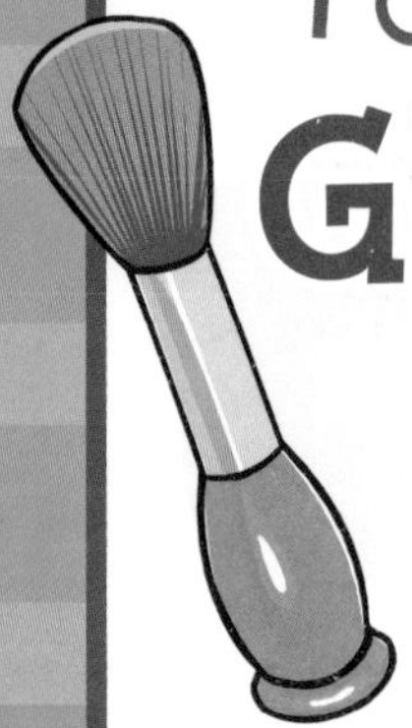

Glamour TIPS

Fashion is about expressing yourself!
Create your own list of "do's" and "don'ts."
Here are a few to get you started!

Do set trends!

Don't be afraid to mix and match patterns!

Do let your personality shine through!

Don't be afraid to stand out in the crowd!

_____

_____

_____

_____

_____

_____

_____

PUPPY LOVE

Fill in the blanks to complete this silly story about owning a puppy. Pick a NOUN, ADJECTIVE, or VERB from the word bank to place in a corresponding blank, or think of your own weird words!

Puppies are a lot of _kitten_ [NOUN]! There are lots of things to

nap [VERB] before you get a puppy—a leash, a crate, and of course,

yummy _treat_ [NOUN]s. Puppies can be big or _purple_ [ADJECTIVE], but

all puppies need lots of love and _apple_ [NOUN]. It's important to

think [VERB] your puppy so it stays _dirty_ [ADJECTIVE] and well–behaved.

Take your puppy to the groomer so its fur doesn't get _small_ [ADJECTIVE].

Make sure to _slip_ [VERB] before getting a puppy—or you may

get more than you bargained for!

WORD BANK

ADJECTIVES	NOUNS	VERBS
small	apple	hug
sweet	bone	buy
long	gumdrop	slip
tangled	snack	jingle
sugary	kitten	nap
hidden	dust	train
purple	work	kick
proud	treat	think
dirty	jump rope	sit

115

How To TIPS

Goofy photographs of your best buds are guaranteed to bring a smile to your face when you are blue. There are many ways to create your funny photo gallery.

Funny Photo Gallery

PRETTY AS A PICTURE

One way to create a photo gallery is by mounting a montage of buddy pics on a bulletin board. Or, you could cut out and hang paper-doll chains with photos or drawings of your friend's faces.

Another idea: decorate each frame to reflect your pictured pal's interests. If one of your friends loves playing softball, have the framed covered with softballs, bats, and helmets. Hang your gallery on your wall so you can admire it!

MINI MASTERPIECE

PICTURE PERFECT

You can also create your own groovy picture frames out of plain, store-bought frames. Paint the frames or apply stickers, fabric, shells, or other materials with glue. Check out your local craft store for miniature items and charms to liven up any frame.

Write Your
Own Story

My idea of a dream vacation is...

What If?

Life can be so serious and routine. It's fun to dream and imagine a different reality! Make a list of the following what-ifs to see what you learn about yourself.

If someone wrote a song about you, what would it be called?

If you had to eliminate one of your senses, which would it be? Why?

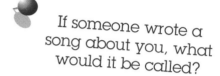

If you had to choose a new name, what you call yourself? Why?

If you could become any animal for a day, which would it be? Why?

If you could be someone else for a day, who would you be?

If you could be an instant expert on anything, what would it be?

Recipes

BLUEBERRY PARFAIT
Snacks

Yogurt parfaits are delicious for breakfast and for a snack. They're also fun to make! If you don't have any blueberries handy, try fruits like strawberries or peaches.

INGREDIENTS & DIRECTIONS

You'll need:

- 1 cup vanilla yogurt
- ½ cup granola
- 1 cup blueberries
- 1 teaspoon maple syrup

Fill two parfait dishes*, glasses, coffee mugs, or bowls with ¼ cup of yogurt. Top each one with 1 teaspoon of the granola. Then add ¼ cup of blueberries. Repeat the layers. Drizzles each parfait with maple syrup.

Makes 2 blueberry yogurt parfaits

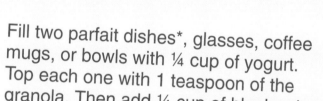

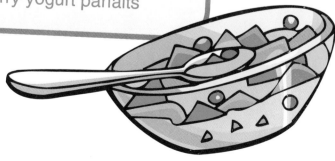

*Ask your parents if you have any allergies.

Manicures
Glamour TIPS

Treat your nails to some tender, loving care with an at-home manicure! Learn the ins and outs of nail care and you'll have a "perfect 10" in no time. Ask an adult for help.

TOUGH AS NAILS

Start by removing any old nail polish. Shape the nail using a file or emery board. Rounded or square nail tips produce strong, beautiful nails.

WARM & BUBBLY

Prepare a warm, soapy bath to soak your hands in for a few minutes. This step softens your cuticles. Using an orangewood stick, clean under the edge of your nails and gently push the cuticle back.

FIRST THINGS FIRST

Apply a base coat of nail polish that includes calcium. This keeps your nails nice and hard, and even helps them grow!

RAINBOW COLORS

After the base coat, apply two coats of your favorite nail polish. Carefully paint your nails without getting your skin colored, too. Allow them to dry for a minute or two—no touching!

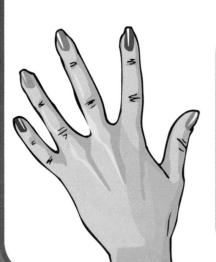

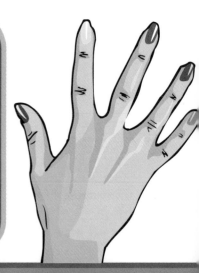

Plan your future manicure! Use this page to plan your next manicure party with your friends.

Who will you be inviting to your party?

_____

_____

_____

_____

What supplies do you need to get?

_____

_____

_____

_____

What color combinations should you try?

_____

_____

_____

_____

Make a list of "themed" manicures, so you know what to wear at the next holiday party.

_____

_____

_____

MAKEUP GLITZ

Use the clues about makeup to complete this crossword puzzle.

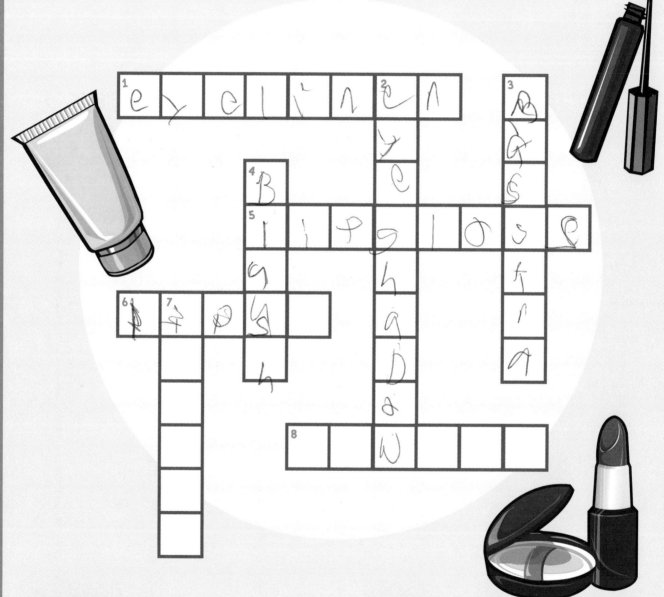

ACROSS
1. Goes around the edges of your eyes
5. Color for your lips
6. Makes your lips shiny
8. Put this on your face with a fluffy pad

DOWN
2. Color for your eyelids
3. Goes on your eyelashes
4. Makes your cheeks rosy
7. Makes your skin soft and smooth

Answer on page 279

WEDDING DRESS STYLES

The most important dress you put on is your wedding dress! Find these types of wedding dress styles in the word search below. Look up, down, backward, forward, and diagonally.

| Ballerina | Column | Halter | Mermaid | Strapless |
| Bead | Empire | Lace | Princess | Sweetheart |

```
E E E B G S G H E Y T I I O
E P E D R R R H S C Z Z G I
Q U Z G D P T T D I B S F C
A W S A N I R E L L A B A H
R S A P R A A I F P S T A F
G L G L P N E M N W E L N L
K O S L G M H R R C T E R O
S E E D I U T I I E E C X N
G S E A P L E F R P M S S N
S D E E O O E R E G M G S A
O B P B P C W E S I R E S H
I D I R A E S D T E K C P A
E E S A P D F H A R H A G U
B I A N I H D E C T W L A P
```

STAR BRIGHT

Are you a super seeker? Put your eyes to the test and see if you can find 10 differences between the picture on the top and the one on the bottom.

Answer on page 279

Doodlin' Biker Chick >>>>>>>>>>>>>>>>>>>>>

Use your imagination to finish designing the wardrobe and accessories for this biker collection.

PROM DRESS

It's time for the prom! Can you find the two pictures that are exactly alike?

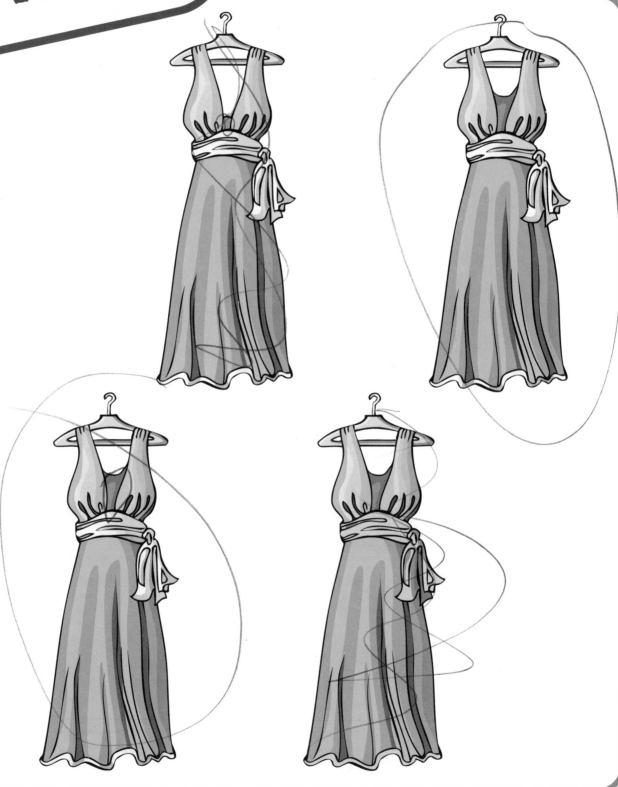

Answer on page 280

LET'S FLY

Clowns (2)   Kangaroo   Rowboat
Flower dress Long skirt Star
Guitar   Mouse   Telescope
              Purple hat

Sudoku
GET HAPPY

Put a little spring into your step and try to decode this sudoku. Fill in the empty squares so that each row, column, and square contains the numbers 1–9 only once.

				9				6
	3	6		2				
2	7		3			4		
	2					5	6	
7					5	2		
5			6	4				9
		2	8	7	3			
	4						8	
8	9	7				6	3	1

Answer on page 280

HOPSCOTCH

Fill in the blanks to complete this silly story about hopscotch. Pick a NOUN, ADJECTIVE, or VERB from the word bank to place in a corresponding blank, or think of your own weird words!

My _cup cakes_ and I usually play hopscotch at
 [NOUN]

cat. We each take turns _play_ ing over
 [NOUN] [VERB]

the squares. Sometimes we _win_ a _sleep_
 [VERB] [ADJECTIVE]

pebble to throw, and other times a _school_. The score
 [NOUN]

is kept on the ground in _serious_ chalk. Jenny usually
 [ADJECTIVE]

crawl s. I wish we got to play this _crinkly_
 [VERB] [ADJECTIVE]

game in _glove_ class!
 [NOUN]

WORD BANK

ADJECTIVES	NOUNS	VERBS
small	gym	jump rope	jump	find
round	friend	basketball	~~win~~	play
colorful	crinkly	school	cat	leap	fall
fun	dull	penny	glove	~~crawl~~	look
crazy	~~serious~~	cupcake		slither	
	sleepy				

Write Your Own Story

Get inspired and write your own story about if you owned a restaurant.

If I owned a restaurant... **?**

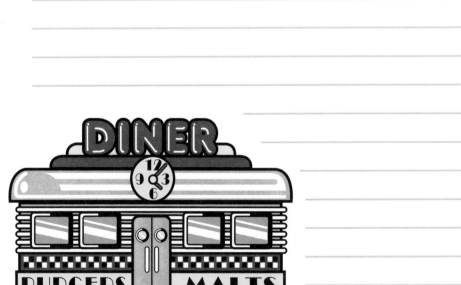

Arts & Crafts Maze

Let's do some arts and crafts! Help this girl make a beautiful necklace by following the correct path through the maze. The correct path is made up of scissors only.

START ↓

FINISH →

Healthy Hair Glamour TIPS

It's important to keep you hair healthy and full of shine. After all, healthy hair reflects a healthy person. Follow these simple tips and your hair will always be in full swing!

GET A TRIM

You hair will look its healthiest with regular trims—around every six weeks.

TAKE CONTROL

Use shampoo and conditioner that is right for your hair. If you have oily hair, try a shampoo that is made for oil control.

DRY WITH CARE

Blow dry only when necessary. This is the prime way girls damage their hair! Use a leave-in conditioner when possible.

LOVE YOUR LOCKS

Brush before bedtime! Make this a habit—brushing will distribute natural oils from root to end. This will make your locks nice and shiny!

COVER UP

Cover your hair when in the sun—it gets sun damaged too! Make sure to wear a hat if you will be outside all day.

List your Friends Forever

Now's the time to celebrate your best friend! Keep a list of the cool things you've done together and what makes you gals a dynamic duo.

Your best friend is...

How would you describe your best friend in five words or less?

You have been best buds since...

What do the two of you have in common?

If you could pick one of you best buds traits, it would be...

How Do You Deal With Surprises?

Do you always do things the same way, or do you like to look for new adventures? Take this quiz to figure out how well you deal with surprises.

Fear · Caution · Enthusiasm

1. You and your best friend always have lunch together on Fridays. One Friday, your bud brings the new girl in school along with her. You—

    a - Be polite, but use some secret signals to let your pal know how upset you are that she brought along an intruder. (4)

    b - Pretend the new girl isn't there and just talk to your bud. (2)

    c - Help the new girl feel welcome by showing her the best places in town to eat. (6)

2. Your parents said that your friend could color your hair with you with her all-natural hair dye. But instead of blonde, it turned out bright orange! You—

    a - Stay home from school until you can change the color. (2)

    b - Wear a sign that says: "My best friend did this to me!" (4)

    c - Pick out an outfit that goes with orange, and act like you planned the whole thing. (6)

3. Your parents take you to your favorite Chinese restaurant. You order your usual, but the waiter brings you some strange dish that you never heard of. You—

    a - Dig in! here's a chance to try a dish that you probably never would have ordered. (6)

    b - Try to swap dishes with one of your parents. (2)

    c - Send it back and watch everybody eat until your food arrives. (4)

4. A family from another country moves in next door. They have a girl your age. You—

    a - Take her some brownies and introduce yourself. Then make a date to visit again, so she can fix you some cool snack food from her country. (6)

    b - Ignore her, since you probably have nothing in common. (4)

    c - Wait to see what she's like in school before you get friendly with her. (2)

5. You're at the movie theater waiting in line for a movie you've been dying to see. The 7:30 showing is sold out and the next one is past your curfew. The only other movie playing now is a black-and-white movie from the 1960's. You—

a - Forget the movies. Instead, go to the ice-cream shop next door and have a big ice-cream sundae with your movie money. (4)

b - Call your parents and ask them to come get you immediately. There's no way you're going to sit through some movie that's over 50 years old. (4)

c - Decide to give the old movie a try since you're already there. There must be some reason it's been around this long. (2)

Fear 10-15 points

You may be surprised to learn that the key to your score is fear. Change seems like a very scary thing to you. The next time something different or unexpected happens, try to think of it as an adventure.

Caution 16-24 points

You sometimes are too cautious and tend to worry too much about what people think of you. Trust yourself more and you'll do fine in new situations.

Enthusiasm 25-30 points

You are eager for new experiences. You like to try new things. Keep it up and you will have many excellent adventures in life!

Recipes

FRESH FRUIT DIPPING DELIGHT

Snacks

This delicious dip is splendidly sweet and wonderfully healthy. It's perfect for an after-school pick-me-up and a fun finger food to entertain your friends.

INGREDIENTS & DIRECTIONS

You'll need:

- 1 container vanilla yogurt

- 1 tablespoon brown sugar

- Apples, peaches, bananas, strawberries, or any of your favorite fruits

Mix brown sugar* and yogurt. Ask your parents to help you cut up the fruit into pieces that are just right for dipping. Dip in!

*Ask your parents if you have any allergies.

BALLET STAR

Arabesque, plié, pirouette! Can you find the two pictures that are exactly alike?

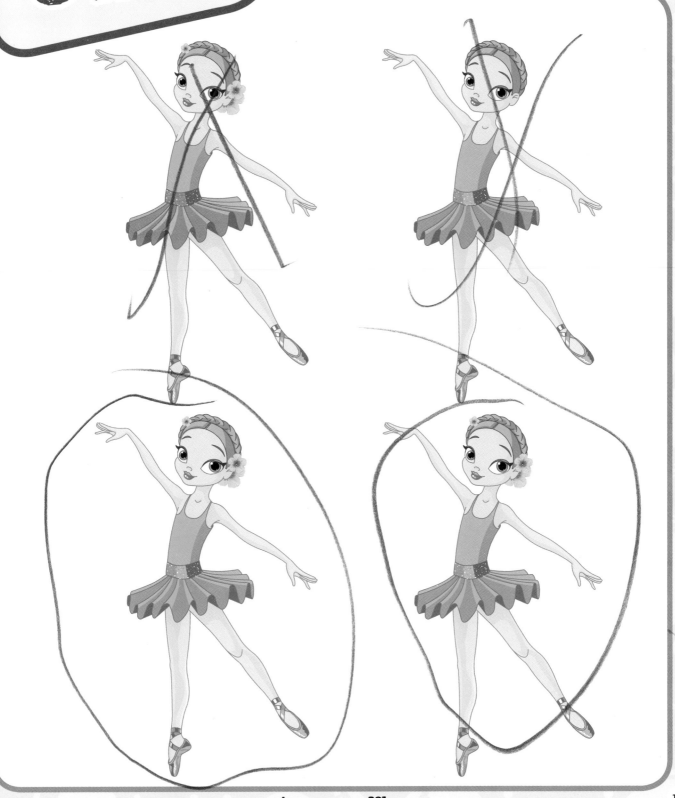

Cool Cats

Are you a super seeker? Put your eyes to the test and see if you can find 10 differences between the picture on the top and the one on the bottom.

How To TIPS

Let's face it: Sometimes, schoolwork can be a drag, but schoolwork and homework are facts of your life. Use these school tips to help you make more time to hang out with friends.

Be a Whiz at School

AVOID PUTTING OFF WORK

The minute the teacher lays out an assignment in class, get to work. The sooner you get started, the sooner you'll finish. It's better to get started right away.

GET ORGANIZED

Take notes as your teachers assign schoolwork and homework. Review your homework notes before you leave school for the day.

KEEP A SCHEDULE

Figure out when you do your best work. It's best if you can get your homework done right away. Find your schedule and keep to it.

Ask your parents if you can have a desk in your room, or use a corner of the dining-room table. Keep all your homework supplies that you might need in that one spot.

MAKE YOURSELF COMFORTABLE

Throw a Makeover Party
Glamour TIPS

Invite your fellow beauty fans over for a night of make-up, hair styling, clothes, and lots of cool looks. Follow this plan to help you prepare. Don't forget to take photos!

Make-up Station Checklist:

- ✓ Eye shadow
- ✓ Mascara
- ___ Mascara wands
- ✓ Lip gloss
- ✓ Lipstick
- ✓ Blush
- ✓ Make-up brushes
- ✓ Make-up remover
- ✓ Tissues
- ___ Extras _____
  _____

Hair-Styling Station Checklist:

- ✓ Hair dryer
- ✓ Combs
- ✓ Brushes
- ___ Hair rollers
- ✓ Hair bands
- ___ Bobby pins
- ✓ Clips
- ✓ Head bands
- ✓ Hair products (hair spray, mousse, gel, etc.)
- ___ Extras _____
  _____

Clothes Station Checklist:

- ___ Scarves
- ___ Hats
- ___ Gloves
- ✓ Jewelry (costume earrings, rings, necklaces, etc)
- ___ Boas
- ___ Vintage dresses
- ___ Extras _____
  _____

Set up each station so that you and your friends visit one station at a time and then rotate. Everyone will visit each station! Tell your friends to get creative—sometimes the wackiest makeovers are the most fun!

Makeover Notes: Remember the highlights!

Who had the most glamorous hairstyle? Describe it!

_____

_____

_____

_____

Who had the most hilarious outfit? Describe it!

_____

_____

_____

_____

Who applied the most memorable make-up? Describe it!

_____

_____

_____

_____

Who had the best all-over makeover? Describe it!

_____

_____

_____

_____

Capricorn
December 22 to January 21

Hey Miss Capricorn!

You're studious and hard-working, Capricorn girl! With your grades and ambitious attitude, you're likely to go far—look out Ivy League, a Cap is headed your way! You surround yourself with friends that support you to help reach your goals. But, listen up: there's more to life than work!

Your Sign	Best Love Match
Goat	Pisces and Scorpio

	Best Friend Match
	Taurus and Virgo

Your Element	Best Fashion Look
Earth	Shoes

Your Flower	Best Colors
Pansy	Black, brown, other dark colors

Lucky Number	Best Careers
11	Engineer, Dentist, Politician

You Know You're a Capricorn If...

Take this quiz to find out if you are a true Capricorn! Check off each question that describes your personality. Tally up the answers (each check mark is worth one point) to find out the results!

1. You love to personalize gifts!

2. You like your privacy!

3. You know the best vintage shops!

4. You can't stand untidy rooms!

5. You don't like surprises!

6. You love to sing!

7. You know what you want!

8. You are an independent gal!

9. You are a reliable friend!

1-3	4-6	7-9
Your personality matches another zodiac sign!	Sure, you're a Capricorn, but you have strong traits of other signs, too!	Hey girl—you are a true Capricorn!

HOROSCOPE

Aquarius

Hey Miss Aquarius!

Check out the latest indie band? Volunteer lately? I'm sure you have, Aquarius girl! You are an independent thinker who likes to form her own opinions, fashion rules, and study habits. You have a sharp mind and quick wit—just don't forget that other people have opinions, too!

Your Sign
Water carrier

Your Element
Water

Your Flower
Birds of Paradise

Lucky Number
27

Best Love Match
Aries and Sagittarius

Best Friend Match
Gemini and Libra

Best Fashion Look
Vintage

Best Colors
Iridescent colors, violet

Best Careers
Social Worker, Aeronautic Engineer, Guidance Counselor

You Know You're an Aquarius If...

Take this quiz to find out if you are a true Aquarius! Check off each question that describes your personality. Tally up the answers (each check mark is worth one point) to find out the results!

1. You don't like quarreling with friends!

2. You might sign up for sky-diving lessons!

3. You like puzzles and riddles!

4. You prefer flip-flops to heels!

5. You are a great planner!

6. You are likely to be famous one day!

7. You can't stand borrowing things!

8. You like the simple life!

9. You get involved in school!

1-3	4-6	7-9
Your personality matches another zodiac sign!	Sure, you're an Aquarius, but you have strong traits of other signs, too!	Hey girl—you are a true Aquarius!

Pisces

February 19 to March 20

Hey Miss Pisces!

You're the best shoulder to cry on, Pisces girl! A caring and compassionate gal like you is always willing to help a friend in need. And being a selfless, sympathetic listener will sometimes make you lose track of time. Keep an eye on the clock—you're always late!

Your Sign
Fish

Your Element
Water

Your Flower
Poppy

Lucky Number
34

Best Love Match
Capricorn and Taurus

Best Friend Match
Cancer and Scorpio

Best Fashion Look
Comfy and casual

Best Colors
Green, dark purple, white

Best Careers
Charitable Organization Leader, Podiatrist, Veterinarian

You Know You're a Pisces If...

Take this quiz to find out if you are a true Pisces! Check off each question that describes your personality. Tally up the answers (each check mark is worth one point) to find out the results!

1. You love healthy foods!

2. You are a great swimmer!

3. You are very romantic!

4. You have a soft spot for poetry!

5. You've mastered the latest yoga move!

6. You are sensitive toward others!

7. You want to be an artist!

8. You like to wear nice jewelry!

9. You need alone time!

1-3	4-6	7-9
Your personality matches another zodiac sign!	Sure, you're a Pisces, but you have strong traits of other signs, too!	Hey girl—you are a true Pisces!

HOROSCOPE

Aries

March 22 to April 21

Hey Miss Aries!

Look out, Aries girl is on the move! Aries is a Fire sign so you're sassy, spunky, adventurous and quick-witted! But, also quick-tempered… check your fiery attitude at the door!

Your Sign

Ram

Your Element

Fire

Your Flower

Tiger Lily

Lucky Number

16

Best Love Match

Gemini and Aquarius

Best Friend Match

Leo and Sagittarius

Best Fashion Look

Boots

Best Colors

Red

Best Careers

Hair Stylist, Artist, Physical Therapist

You Know You're an Aries If...

Take this quiz to find out if you are a true Aries! Check off each question that describes your personality. Tally up the answers (each check mark is worth one point) to find out the results!

1. You think staying home on a Friday night is boring!

2. You never leave home without your lipgloss!

3. You are the first in line to ride the roller coaster!

4. You love standing out in a crowd!

5. You wear lots of bright colors!

6. You look great in hats!

7. You hate to be ignored!

8. You hardly ever take someone else's advice!

9. You love red roses!

1-3	4-6	7-9
Your personality matches another zodiac sign!	Sure, you're an Aries, but you have strong traits of other signs, too!	Hey girl—you are a true Aries!

Taurus

April 22 to May 21

Hey Miss Taurus!

Your symbol is the Bull, Miss Taurus—perfect since you can be a bit stubborn at times! But mostly, you're athletic and love to shop!

Your Sign

Bull

Your Element

Earth

Your Flower

Rose

Lucky Number

12

Best Love Match

Pisces and Cancer

Best Friend Match

Virgo and Capricorn

Best Fashion Look

Necklaces and scarves

Best Colors

Gold and pastels

Best Careers

Actress, Banker, Fashion PR

You Know You're a Taurus If...

Take this quiz to find out if you are a true Taurus! Check off each question that describes your personality. Tally up the answers (each check mark is worth one point) to find out the results!

1. Dinner is your favorite meal!

2. You like natural ingredients!

3. You love luxury!

4. You can't stand being indoors!

5. You like to take your time!

6. You can stretch a dollar!

7. You know how to accessorize!

8. You are a hardworker!

9. You really, really don't like to be interrupted!

1-3	4-6	7-9
Your personality matches another zodiac sign!	Sure, you're a Taurus, but you have strong traits of other signs, too!	Hey girl—you are a true Taurus!

HOROSCOPE

Gemini

May 22 to June 21

Hey Miss Gemini!

You're a social butterfly who dabbles in loads of different hobbies. But, be careful or you'll look like a busy bee when it comes to sticking your nose in other people's business—lucky for you, your quick wit will get you out of any sticky situation.

Your Sign

Twin

Best Love Match

Aries and Leo

Best Friend Match

Aquarius and Libra

Your Element

Air

Best Fashion Look

Accessories

Your Flower

Orchid

Best Colors

Shades of blue

Lucky Number

15

Best Careers

Writer, Postal Officer, Television Host

You Know You're a Gemini If...

Take this quiz to find out if you are a true Gemini! Check off each question that describes your personality. Tally up the answers (each check mark is worth one point) to find out the results!

 1. You hate waiting!

 2. You have a short attention span!

 3. You love to read!

 4. You are a multi-tasker!

 5. You love being around people!

 6. You like to travel!

 7. You have a full social calendar!

 8. You are moody!

 9. You are always late!

1-3	4-6	7-9
Your personality matches another zodiac sign!	Sure, you're a Gemini, but you have strong traits of other signs, too!	Hey girl—you are a true Gemini!

HOROSCOPE

Cancer

June 22 to July 21

Hey Miss Cancer!

A quiet night at home? Sounds just about right for a Cancer girl. You love taking care of your friends, and appreciate the little things in life (like mani-pedis!). It's also good that you're kind and devoted… you'll probably have a big family one day!

Your Sign
Crab

Your Element
Water

Your Flower
Lily

Lucky Number
32

Best Love Match
Taurus and Virgo

Best Friend Match
Pisces and Scorpio

Best Fashion Look
Cotton shirts and pants

Best Colors
Orange-yellow and blue-green

Best Careers
Nurse, Nutritionist, Interior Designer

You Know You're a Cancer If...

Take this quiz to find out if you are a true Cancer! Check off each question that describes your personality. Tally up the answers (each check mark is worth one point) to find out the results!

1. You enjoy quiet time!

2. You are a great babysitter!

3. You give big hugs!

4. You love gourmet food!

5. You don't like to be criticized!

6. You are caring!

7. You like to be comfy!

8. You throw super parties!

9. You are not good under pressure!

1-3	4-6	7-9
Your personality matches another zodiac sign!	Sure, you're a Cancer, but you have strong traits of other signs, too!	Hey girl—you are a true Cancer!

HOROSCOPE

Leo

July 23 to August 22

Hey Miss Leo!

You, Lion girl, like to be the center of attention! That means that you never have a hair out of place and are always surrounded by lots of friends—and are most likely the leader of the pack. Watch out: you can be bossy!

Your Sign

Lion

Your Element

Fire

Your Flower

Sunflower

Lucky Number

44

Best Love Match

Gemini and Libra

Best Friend Match

Sagittarius and Aries

Best Fashion Look

Bold prints

Best Colors

Gold and fiery red

Best Careers

Actress, Fashion Stylist, Party Planner

You Know You're a Leo If...

Take this quiz to find out if you are a true Leo! Check off each question that describes your personality. Tally up the answers (each check mark is worth one point) to find out the results!

1. You stay away from mean people!

2. You love pets!

3. You are creative!

4. You like to be complimented!

5. You look for adventure!

6. You don't know how to save money!

7. You are cool under pressure!

8. You are loyal!

9. You make your friends laugh!

1-3	4-6	7-9
Your personality matches another zodiac sign!	Sure, you're a Leo but you have strong traits of other signs, too!	Hey girl—you are a true Leo!

HOROSCOPE

Virgo

August 23 to September 22

Hey Miss Virgo!

Is that a list you're making? If you're like any other Virgo girl, you like things neat and organized. You get great grades and are an athletic superstar. Remember: even though you're shy, come out of your shell once in a while!

Your Sign
The Female

Your Element
Earth

Your Flower
Chrysanthemum

Lucky Number
27

Best Love Match
Cancer and Scorpio

Best Friend Match
Taurus and Capricorn

Best Fashion Look
Tailored shirts, pants, and dresses

Best Colors
Violet and teal

Best Careers
Illustrator, Editor, Accountant

You Know You're a Virgo If...

Take this quiz to find out if you are a true Virgo! Check off each question that describes your personality. Tally up the answers (each check mark is worth one point) to find out the results!

1. You don't like crowded, noisy places!

2. You stay away from wearing bright colors!

3. You love to win!

4. You are very helpful!

5. You are looking for true love!

6. You like things organized!

7. You are a health fanatic!

8. You reach your goals!

9. You worry!

1-3	4-6	7-9
Your personality matches another zodiac sign!	Sure, you're a Virgo, but you have strong traits of other signs, too!	Hey girl—you are a true Virgo!

HOROSCOPE

Libra

September 23
to October 22

Hey Miss Libra!

If anyone is going to know the latest styles and trends… it's you, Libra girl! You are the fashionista and peacemaker of your group. You love surrounding yourself with beautiful things (including boys!) and love to look stunning—just be careful not to get caught up in the superficial stuff!

Your Sign
Scale

Your Element
Air

Your Flower
Daisy

Lucky Number
8

Best Love Match
Leo and Sagittarius

Best Friend Match
Aquarius and Libra

Best Fashion Look
The latest trend

Best Colors
Red and yellow

Best Careers
Fashion Stylist, Florist, Fine Art Dealer

You Know You're a Libra If...

Take this quiz to find out if you are a true Libra! Check off each question that describes your personality. Tally up the answers (each check mark is worth one point) to find out the results!

1. You can shop till you drop!

2. You are a social butterfly!

3. You are sensible!

4. You can be a flirt!

5. You love to share!

6. You will dance the night away!

7. You prefer floral-scented perfume!

8. You don't like bad manners!

9. You are well-balanced!

1-3	4-6	7-9
Your personality matches another zodiac sign!	Sure, you're a Libra, but you have strong traits of other signs, too!	Hey girl—you are a true Libra!

HOROSCOPE

Scorpio

October 23 to November 21

Hey Miss Scorpio!

Who is that mysterious, secretive girl reading in the window seat? It's got to be you, Scorpio girl! You love to explore through books and magazines and are solid as a rock—no flakiness here! While you like to be alone, you also like the company of others and almost always have a boyfriend, just don't let him see your moody side!

Your Sign

Scorpion

Your Element

Water

Your Flower

Gardenia

Lucky Number

7

Best Love Match

Capricorn and Virgo

Best Friend Match

Pisces and Cancer

Best Fashion Look

Knee-high boots and stilettos

Best Colors

Dark browns and dark reds

Best Careers

Pharmacist, Private Investigator, Surgeon

You Know You're a Scorpio If...

Take this quiz to find out if you are a true Scorpio! Check off each question that describes your personality. Tally up the answers (each check mark is worth one point) to find out the results!

1. You are embarrassed by too many compliments!

2. You never tell a secret!

3. You dislike lies!

4. You'll never have enough shoes!

5. You are protective of your friends!

6. You'd rather stay home than travel!

7. You love mystery books!

8. You are great at sports!

9. You carefully spend your money!

1-3	4-6	7-9
Your personality matches another zodiac sign!	Sure, you're a Scorpio, but you have strong traits of other signs, too!	Hey girl—you are a true Scorpio!

Sagittarius
November 22 to December 21

Hey Miss Sagittarius!

Who wants to have fun, fun, FUN? You, Sagittarius girl, are always looking for a party. People love to be around you. And why not? Your boundless energy and happy-go-lucky point of view makes you the most fun pal to be around.

Your Sign
Archer

Your Element
Fire

Your Flower
Carnation

Lucky Number
24

Best Love Match
Aquarius and Libra

Best Friend Match
Leo and Aries

Best Fashion Look
Sunglasses, jeans, and leather jackets

Best Colors
Green, purple, white

Best Careers
Teacher, Flight Attendant, Radio DJ

You Know You're a Sagittarius If...

Take this quiz to find out if you are a true Sagittarius! Check off each question that describes your personality. Tally up the answers (each check mark is worth one point) to find out the results!

1. You want to travel the world one day!

2. You like comfortable and stylish clothes!

3. You have tons of friends!

4. You never leave home without sunglasses!

5. You're the first to know the newest band!

6. You are a risk taker!

7. You love your freedom!

8. You can't stand to be confined!

9. You'll buy a lottery ticket!

1-3	4-6	7-9
Your personality matches another zodiac sign!	Sure, you're a Sagittarius, but you have strong traits of other signs, too!	Hey girl—you are a true Sagittarius!

January

Fill in the calendar with all of the January birthdays you don't want to forget.

1	2	3	4	5	6 S¡s B-Day	7
8	9	10	11	12	13	14
15	16	17	18	19	20	21
22	23	24	25	26	27	28
29	30	31				

To Do:

_____

_____

_____

February

Fill in the calendar with all of the February birthdays you don't want to forget.

1	2	3	4	5	6	7
8	9	10	11	12	13	14
15	16	17	18	19	20	21
22	23	24	25	26	27	28
29						

To Do:

_____

_____

_____

March

Fill in the calendar with all of the March birthdays you don't want to forget.

1	2	3	4	5	6	7
8	9	10	11	12	13	14
15	16	17	18	19	20	21
22	23	24	25	26	27	28
29	30	31				

To Do:

_____

_____

_____

April

Fill in the calendar with all of the April birthdays you don't want to forget.

1	2	3	4	5	6	7
8	9	10	11	12	13	14
15	16	17	18	19	20	21
22	23	24	25	26	27	28
29	30					

To Do:
_____
_____
_____

May

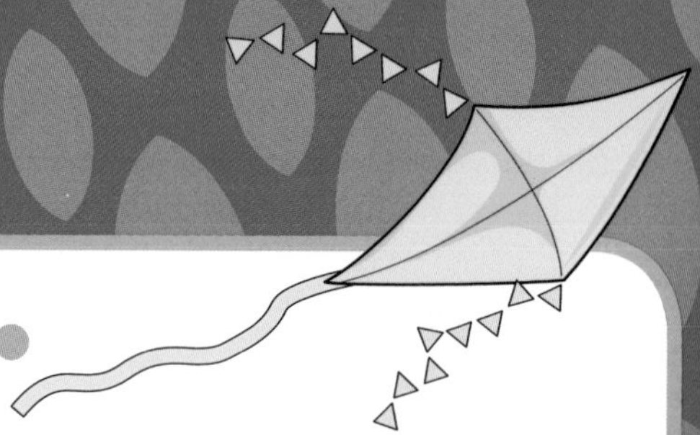

Fill in the calendar with all of the May birthdays you don't want to forget.

1	2	3	4	5	6	7
8	9	10	11	12	13	14
15	16	17	18	19	20	21
22	23	24	25	26	27	28
29	30	31				

To Do:

_____

_____

_____

June

Fill in the calendar with all of the June birthdays you don't want to forget.

1	2	3	4	5	6	7
8	9	10	11	12	13	14
15	16	17	18	19	20	21
22	23	24	25	26	27	28
29	30					

To Do:
_____

_____

_____

July

Fill in the calendar with all of the July birthdays you don't want to forget.

1	2	3	4	5	6	7
8	9	10	11	12	13	14
15	16	17	18	19	20	21
22	23	24	25	26	27	28
29	30	31				

To Do:

_____

_____

_____

August

Fill in the calendar with all of the August birthdays you don't want to forget.

1	2	3	4	5	6	7
8	9	10	11	12	13	14
15	16	17	18	19	20	21
22	23	24	25	26	27	28
29	30	31				

To Do:

_____

_____

_____

September

WELCOME!

Fill in the calendar with all of the September birthdays you don't want to forget.

1	2	3	4	5	6	7
8	9	10	11	12	13	14
15	16	17	18	19	20	21
22	23	24	25	26	27	28
29	30					

To Do:

_____

_____

_____

October

Fill in the calendar with all of the October birthdays you don't want to forget.

1	2	3	4	5	6	7
8	9	10	11	12	13	14
15	16	17	18	19	20	21
22	23	24	25	26	27	28
29	30	31				

To Do:

_____

_____

_____

November

Fill in the calendar with all of the November birthdays you don't want to forget.

1	2	3	4	5	6	7
8	9	10	11	12	13	14
15	16	17	18	19	20	21
22	23	24	25	26	27	28
29	30					

To Do:

December

Fill in the calendar with all of the December birthdays you don't want to forget.

1	2	3	4	5	6	7
8	9	10	11	12	13	14
15	16	17	18	19	20	21
22	23	24	25	26	27	28
29	30	31				

To Do:

_____

_____

_____

How To TIPS

Friendship Scrapbook

If you like craft projects, you'll have a blast making your own friendship scrapbook. You probably already have lots of photos, invitations, and ticket stubs that remind you of all the fun things you've done with your friends.

FIRST THINGS FIRST

Start your project with a large binder. Some craft stores sell binders designed specifically to hold pictures. Decorate the front and back of your binder with stickers, photos, lace, velvet, ribbons, and markers.

INSIDE OUT

Now that you have the outside decorated, it's time to get to work with the inside. A good idea is to organize your scrapbook chronologically or by theme.

CUSTOM TOUCHES

After you finished one of the binders, you may notice that you want to add more pictures. You can always go back to a craft store or you can make your own custom ones.

MEMORY LANE

You can pull out the friendship scrapbook and look at it whenever you need cheering up or a good laugh. Take a stroll down memory lane and think about all the good times you had!

What does your ...

Handwriting

... Say about you?

Follow this chart to figure out the personality your handwriting reveals. At the end, you'll find a description that just might perfectly describe you!

Start

Your perfect day is to be:
- Outdoors
- Indoors

You're most likely to be found:
- Chilling with friends
- Shopping

What kind of perfume do you like?
- Spicy
- Floral
- Sweet

Your favorite sport is:
- Cheerleading
- Soccer
- Softball

Which way does your handwriting slope?
- Downward
- Upward

Where do you like to write?
- In bed
- On the deck

What size is your handwriting?
- Large
- Small

ADVENTUROUS
Your bold handwriting and preference to be outdoors proves that your adventurous spirit always shines through!

SOCIAL
You love to play sports and be with friends—and your large, upward-sloping handwriting tells the world just how much of a social butterfly you are!

COMPASSIONATE
Your calm disposition and small penmanship is a sign that you are compassionate and a reliable friend!

179

BASKETBALL STAR

Fill in the blanks to complete this silly story about basketball. Pick a NOUN, ADJECTIVE, or VERB from the word bank to place in a corresponding blank, or think of your own weird words!

One day, I want to play _Happy_ [ADJECTIVE] basketball. People all

over the _pumpkin_ [NOUN] would watch me _create_ [VERB] points.

I would be the _sleepy_ [ADJECTIVE] player on the _math_ [NOUN] !

Everyone would try to _bake_ [VERB] the ball just like me. One

day, my _sandy_ [ADJECTIVE] jersey will _slice_ [VERB] in the hall of

fame. But before that, I have a lot of _popsicle_ [NOUN] to do.

WORD BANK

ADJECTIVES
best
old
~~sandy~~
clingy
professional
wet
~~happy~~
~~sleepy~~
loud

NOUNS
world
team
practice
moon
homework
popsicle
parrot
~~pumpkin~~
~~math~~

VERBS
score
shoot
hang
lug
slice
~~create~~
~~bake~~
draw
lock

BFF StuFF

Are you a super seeker? Put your eyes to the test and see if you can find 10 differences between the picture on the top and the one on the bottom.

TROPICAL GETAWAYS

Vacation trips are a great way to explore new places. Find these tropical getaways in the word search below. Look up, down, backward, forward, and diagonally.

Aruba	Bali	Bora Bora	Fiji	Jamaica
Bahamas	Barbados	Curacao	Hawaii	Virgin Islands

```
A S R E T S C S E P I I J I
A N D C N N O S Y D T B F E
Z R Q N J D M H E S N T F E
S F O S A S A M A H A B C S
B M I B M L L K G H Z S Q T
S A R J A E S O Q B T L Y S
B A L X I R C I T L N J A D
B O R I C T O T N I I D T I
S K J E A A H B N I P M N K
R S S T C R W K A S G R Q J
N G I A M S Y W A B U R A Q
S I R A P I A S E G E E I S
H U T O D H E D C O C N S V
C U B O T J A O I D E E J S
```

Answer on page 281

Up, Up, and Away
Glamour TIPS

Need a lift? Shake things up with a fun and easy updo! Try this side ponytail for any occasion.

YOU'LL NEED

- Comb
- Flat brush
- Hair band
- Bobby pins
- Hair spray

Start by teasing hair at the crown of your head. Then lightly brush to smooth all fly-away strands. Sweep hair into a ponytail, securing it on one side of your head. Wrap a strand of hair around the base of the ponytail to hide the hair band. Tuck the ends back with your bobby pins. Give your side ponytail a light spritz of hair spray.

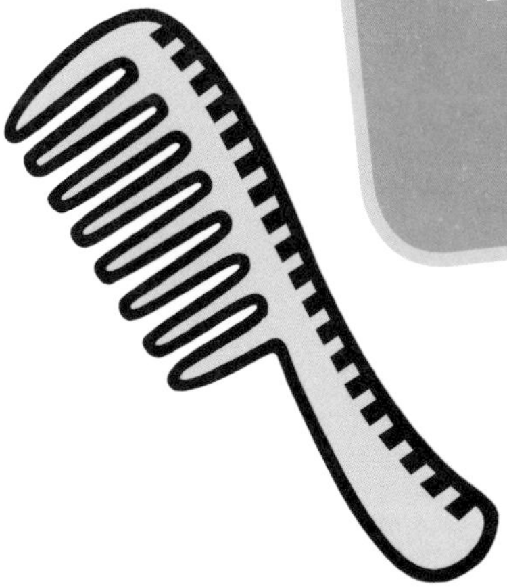

List your
Fashion Designer

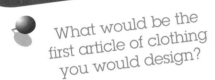

Do your friends flock to you for fashion tips? Are you up to date on all the latest trends? Make a list of the items you would design if you were a fashion designer!

Who are your inspirations?

What would be the first article of clothing you would design?

What would your design label be called?

What does your signature outfit look like?

What styles are your favorites?

184

LAST-MINUTE GROCERIES

Search, find, and circle these 10 things.

Bluebirds (2)　　Fish　　Pink hair bow
Cake　　Nail polish　　Ring
Eight ball　　Pearl necklace　　UFO
Penguin

Answer on page 282

Unicorn Maze

Follow the path from **Start** to **Finish** to help the magical unicorn get to the girl at the end. Make sure the unicorn isn't tempted with treats along the way.

START

FINISH

Answer on page 282

Doodlin' >>>>>>>>>>>>>>>>>>>>>>>>>

Skate Girl

Use your imagination to finish designing this skateboard.

Recipes

SUPER STUFFED PITA POCKETS

Snacks

Look no further for a quick bite to eat that will really fill you up! These pita pockets will do the trick! They contain all sorts of delicious and nutritious vegetables.

INGREDIENTS & DIRECTIONS

You'll need:

- ½ whole wheat pita

- Hummus

- All of your favorite veggies: cucumbers, green and red peppers, carrots, tomatoes

Spread the hummus* inside the pita pocket. Ask for help slicing the veggies, then layer them on the hummus. Delicious!

*Ask your parents if you have any allergies.

Sudoku
WINTER WALK

Take a walk on the wild side and try to decode this sudoku. Fill in the empty squares so that each row, column, and square contains the numbers 1–9 only once.

			8		6		5	
	4			7		3		
8	5			3			2	
2						4		
				4	7			
		3	2		9	7		8
7		5		6				
4		6	7	9	2	8		
				5	3			6

Fabulous Facials
Glamour TIPS

Sometimes you need a little pick-me-up, and what better way to perk up than with a skin-soothing facial? Keep your face fresh and clean with this cool facial tip!

SWEET AS HONEY

Looking to soften up your dry skin? Combine these simple items and you'll be on your way to smoother and silkier skin.

- ¼ cup honey
- 2 tablespoons milk
- 1 teaspoon finely ground almonds

Mix thoroughly and spread over your face. (Be sure to keep it away from your eyes!) Let the mixture set for 10 minutes. After 10 minutes, rinse with cool water and pat dry.

You'll have a sunny outlook on life with these cool shades. Can you find the two pictures that are exactly alike?

Are You Best Friend Material?

You would do absolutely anything for your best friend, right? Put yourself to the test and see how good a friend you would be in these ultra-sticky situations.

Honest Chick · Close Friend · Best Bud

1. **Your best friend has a crush—on the same guy you do! She has asked you to talk to him and find out if he likes her. What do you do?**
   - a – You get "uncrushed" on your sweetheart and talk to him on behalf of your best friend. (2)
   - **b** – You have a heart-to-heart with your best friend and work through the problem. (3)
   - c – You talk to your crush—flirt with him actually—and never mention your best friend. After all, you knew him first! (1)

2. **Your best friend has just bought a new dress for a fancy family occasion. She absolutely loves it. Problem is, you think it's ugly. What do you do?**
   - **a** – You take a deep breath, then gently tell her the truth. (3)
   - b – You tell her not to bother leaving the house. (1)
   - c – You tell her she looks stunning, so as to not hurt her feelings. (2)

3. **Your best friend has just returned your MP3 player after she borrowed it. When you turn it on, you notice something is not right. What do you do?**
   - **a** – You call your friend and ask her if something happened to it. (3)
   - b – You call your friend and yell at her for breaking your MP3 player. (1)
   - c – You don't say anything about it, but you decide never to lend her anything valuable again. (2)

4. **You're out with your family on a Friday night when you spot your best friend's boyfriend with a pretty girl you've never seen before. What do you do?**
   - a – You slip away from the table and call your friend. (1)
   - b – You call her when you get home, sad to break the bad news, but happy to provide emotional support. (3)
   - **c** – You see her the next day and don't mention a word about it so as to not hurt her feelings. (2)

5. During lunch, you overhear two girls gossiping about your best friend. You know your best friend likes these particular girls. What do you do?

a - You stick up for your friend in front of the two girls, then don't mention a word of what happened to your friend. (2)

b - You run back and tell your friend what the girls said about her—even if it hurts her feelings. (1)

c - You tell your friend to stay clear of those girls because they like to talk behind a person's back. (3)

Honest Chick 5-8 points

If you scored 5 to 8 points, you're a little rough around the edges. You are usually honest with your friends, but a little insensitive. Remember that part of a healthy friendship is being kind and offering your friend support.

Close Friend 9-11 points

If you scored 9 to 11 points, you're a good friend overall. However, you sometimes sacrifice the truth for what you believe is kindness. Keep in mind that close friends are honest friends.

Best Bud 12-15 points

If you scored 12 to 15 points, you really know how to communicate with your best bud! When something is bothering you, you let her know. When she's in a tight spot, you help her out. Keep up the good work!

Let's Draw a
Spaniel Puppy

On a separate piece of paper, follow these simple steps using a pencil and an eraser.

1 This cute puppy starts out with these simple shapes. The top oval will be his head, lightly pencil in the nose and muzzle shapes.

2 Now that you have the basic shape roughed in, you can sketch in the puppy's tail, legs, and paws. Then, add the ears and begin to detail the rest of the puppy's face.

3 Add important details like the pup's fur, whiskers, and tongue. Keep adding little details until your puppy looks complete.

4 Once your puppy sketch is finished, add color and shading to really bring your drawing to life. Your Spaniel is ready for adventure!

SALON DAY

Fill in the blanks to complete this silly story about a trip to the salon. Pick a NOUN, ADJECTIVE, or VERB from the word bank to place in a corresponding blank, or think of your own weird words!

For my __Truck__, I get to go to the salon! First, my
[NOUN]

__Bradi__ is __Crayzing__ed and cut. The shampoo
[NOUN]   [VERB]

smells so __Butiegl__. Next, I get my __Watov__s painted.
[ADJECTIVE]   [NOUN]

I choose a __sasory__ color, and the paint takes just a
[ADJECTIVE]

minute to __SDing__. The same color goes on my toes—it's
[VERB]

so __Pretty__! I __Running__ in front of the mirror to check
[ADJECTIVE]   [VERB]

out my __Stink__ look. I look and feel gorgeous!
[ADJECTIVE]

WORD BANK

ADJECTIVES
fruity
bright   quiet
sparkly   wacky
new   nice
muddy   bold

NOUNS
birthday   shoe
hair   ice cream
nail   doll
elbow   notebook
eyebrow

VERBS
wash   pinch
look   swivel
stand   lift
beam   hover
crimp

Doodlin' >>>>>>>>>>>>>>>>>>>>>>>
Tropical Getaway

Use your imagination to finish designing the summer wardrobe and accessories for this tropical collection.

Write Your
Own Story

Get inspired and write your own story about your Hollywood hunk.

My Hollywood hunk is...

Love Bug

Are you a super seeker? Put your eyes to the test and see if you can find 10 differences between the picture on the left and the one on the right.

Answer on page 283

• List your Rockin' Karaoke Tunes

After a long week at school, it's fun to mix it up with a karaoke night. Be prepared when your BFFs come over with a list of go-to tunes.

What songs have a great dance beat to them?

What songs make you think about your friends?

What songs are guaranteed crowd pleasers?

What songs make you want to sing and shout?

What songs would you like to dedicate to your beau?

Recipes

CHEESY PRETZEL DIPPERS
Snacks

Spice up your afternoon with a zesty snack!
These cheese dippers have loads of calcium that
helps keep your bones and teeth healthy and strong.

INGREDIENTS & DIRECTIONS

You'll need:

- **Cubes of cheese**
- **Pretzel sticks**
- **Honey mustard**

Insert pretzel sticks* into cheese cubes. Dip cubes into honey mustard. Say cheese!

*Ask your parents if you have any allergies.

How To TIPS

Learn how to help others and help yourself, too! Use these suggestions to give you some ideas for projects that you might want to tackle.

Community Involvement

FEED ANIMALS AT THE POUND

Are you and your friends animal lovers? A local pound or animal shelter might be the perfect place to pitch in. Many of the animals there need to be walked, bathed, fed, and played with. The animals will love you for it!

CLEAN A PARK

Is there a nearby park that needs a thorough cleanup? Call the local parks and recreation department or town council. Find out if you and your pals can volunteer to clean the park.

Some elderly people live in nursing homes, and they would love to receive hand-made gifts. Several weeks before the holidays, get your buds together and have a card-making party.

Happy Holidays!

MAKE HOLIDAY CARDS

Sweet Tooth

Using the pictures below, complete this rebus puzzle about something that will satisfy your sweet tooth.

-EESE + O +

-L-R + **-NT**

-S -H -L -BUS +

-S -R + S

(handwritten notes on image): cheese, chocoent, chooe, teat, Cloclot, Chocoent

ACCESSORIES

Add some glam to your wardrobe. Find these types of accessories in the word search. Look up, down, backward, forward, and diagonally.

Anklet	Earrings	Necklace	Purse	Sunglasses
Bracelet	Headband	Pin	Ring	Watch

```
G C E I C S N I P S S L S G
S E S S A L G N U S Y X N E
R N Y T D P K I R T S I O A
F S R D A H G T S L R P S A
F S A N I S E M E H A G E A
Z G E O E L B A E E X V Q G
H N O E E R R J D W C A K M
R I X C H C T A W B O M A B
Q R A A M E E B T J A S M T
L R O L L O O E A T L N J P
B A H K P T N L E D I F D E
A E N C R U Y W R E N B A W
C A K E U L I B W E F R Q D
E T E N S P J C M O E C T I
```

Answer on page 283

PET STORE

Fill in the blanks to complete this silly story about a pet store. Pick a NOUN, ADJECTIVE, or VERB from the word bank to place in a corresponding blank, or think of your own weird words!

The pet store is a _____ place—the birds _____,
[ADJECTIVE]   [VERB]

the dogs _____, and people have to shout over the noise.
[VERB]

The _____s munch quietly on carrots. Some animals need a
[NOUN]

_____ place to be, like lizards. Some people get grossed out
[ADJECTIVE]

because lizards eat _____s! The fish live in _____s
[NOUN]   [NOUN]

with clean and _____ water. Be sure to pick up something
[ADJECTIVE]

for your special pet before _____ing the store!
[VERB]

WORD BANK

ADJECTIVES
loud
dark   huge
fresh   flat
smooth spiky
scaly   round

NOUNS
rabbit
bug   house
tank   rock
cow   guitar
ant   purse

VERBS
squawk throw
bark   email
purr   pick
exit   paint
scream

How Healthy are your Habits?

Unhealthy · Balanced · Athletic

1. **It's the first day of summer vacation and the weather is beautiful. You celebrate the new season by:**
    - **a** - Watching TV. After all, it's vacation. (5)
    - **b** - Organizing a softball game in your neighborhood. (15)
    - **c** - Walking over to a friend's house to hang out. (10)

2. **You're sitting down to watch your favorite prime-time show. You are most likely snacking on:**
    - **a** - Potato chips or ice cream (5)
    - **b** - Popcorn or pretzels (10)
    - **c** - Fruit or raw veggies (15)

3. **It's a hot day and the AC is cranking. When your friend calls to see if you would like to go swimming, you:**
    - **a** - Sit under a pool umbrella and watch her swim. (10)
    - **b** - Slip on your swimsuit and run over to the pool. (15)
    - **c** - Say, "No thanks," and turn up the AC. (5)

4. **The first balanced meal you eat each day is:**
    - **a** - Breakfast (15)
    - **b** - Dinner (5)
    - **c** - Lunch (10)

5. **Your favorite sport is:**
    - **a** - Video game (5)
    - **b** - Basketball (15)
    - **c** - Table tennis (10)

Unhealthy 25-30 points

If you scored 25 to 30 points, you need to make some more "active" changes. You may think that it's boring or uncool to be healthy, but you're missing out on a lot of fun! It's time to get off the couch and start making smart food and exercise choices.

Balanced 35-40 points

If you scored 35 to 40 points, you have a well-balanced lifestyle. You take good care of your body and do other fun things, too. You sometimes eat sweets or avoid exercise, but you don't go overboard.

Athletic 45-50 points

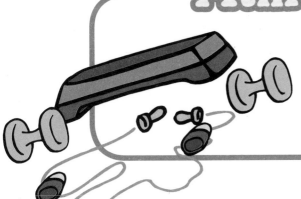

If you scored 45 to 50 points, you are probably very athletic and fit. You know that a healthy body helps you feel great about yourself and have fun.

Fabulous Facials
Glamour TIPS

Keep your oily skin at bay with this oil-fighting skin concoction. This wild oats facial smells great, too!

WILD CHILD

You'll Need:

- ½ cup cooked oatmeal
- 1 teaspoon lemon juice
- ½ cup mashed apple

Mix ingredients into a smooth paste. Apply mixture to your face and wait 15 minutes. Rinse with cool water and pat dry.

RAINBOW BRIGHT

Rainbows are so beautiful! Can you find the two pictures that are exactly alike?

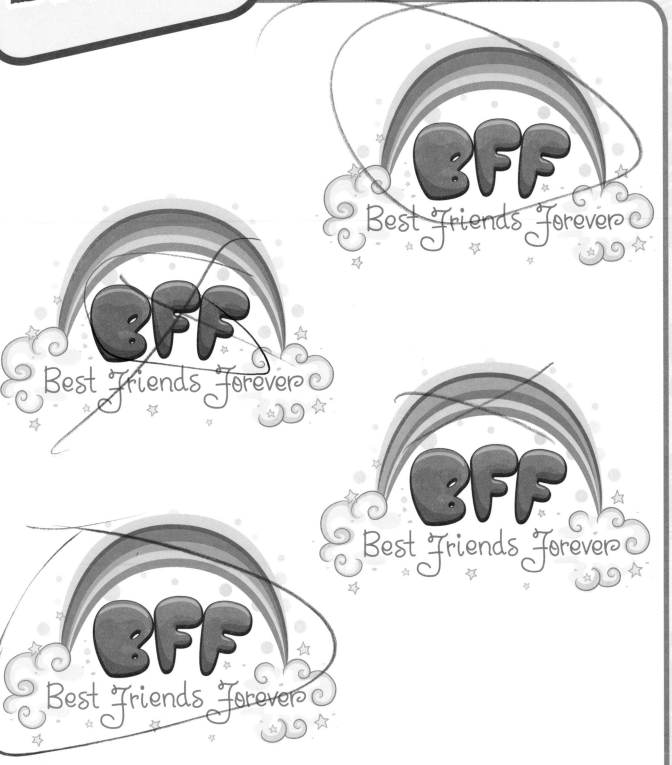

Answer on page 283

PARTY FUN

Use the clues about party items to complete this crossword puzzle.

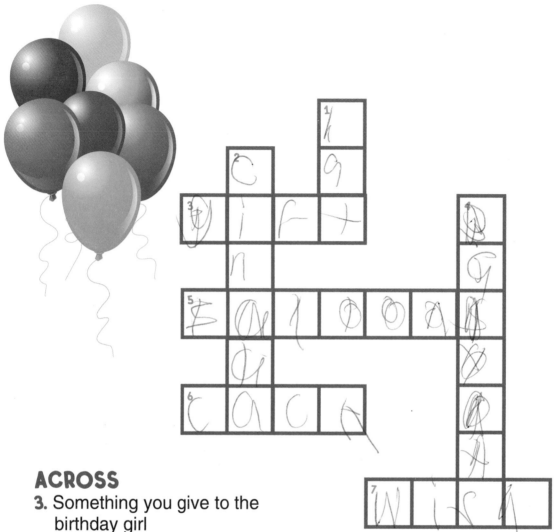

ACROSS

3. Something you give to the birthday girl
5. It's full of hot air.
6. You cover it with icing
7. Blow out the candles and make a _____.

DOWN

1. You wear it on your head
2. It's hung up with a string, and you hit it with a bat.
4. The number of _____ shows how old you are.

Answer on page 284

List your

Girl Zone

Let's face it. Girls are better than boys at certain things! Make a list of things that show how special you are.

 What makes you a super cool girl?

  What's the best thing about being a girl?

 What do you most like about your personality?

 What would you never change about yourself?

 What are you better at than most boys?

How To TIPS

Remember Your Dreams

Dreams are so cool because you can live other lives. Dying to remember your dreams? Check out these great tips.

FAB FIVE

To remember your dreams, it helps to know that you sleep in five stages. The majority of dreams happen in the later stages of sleep. Your brain stays pretty busy while you are sleeping!

POWER OF SUGGESTION

Before you sleep, tell yourself that you will remember your dreams. Say, "Tonight I'm going to remember my dreams." Close your eyes slowly and clear your head.

KEEP A DREAM JOURNAL

When you wake up in the morning, write down any dreams you can remember. You can't remember any dreams? Write down whatever comes into your head to help get you going.

DON'T SKIMP ON SLEEP

You should always try to get a good night's sleep—at least eight hours. Don't cheat yourself out of an awesome night of dreaming!

Write Your

Own Story

If I could have anything, my wish list would include...

?

Doodlin' >>>>>>>>>>>>>>>>>>>>>>>>>>
Geek Chic

Use your imagination to finish designing the wardrobe for this geek chic collection.

TOP SHOPS

Search, find, and circle these 10 things.

Blue headband
Cow
Dogs (3)

Heart
Mouse
Pig
Pigtails

Purple purse
Spotted blouse
Zebra

Hiking Trip Maze

Time to go hiking! Help this girl get to her tent by following the correct path through the maze. The correct path is made up of canteens only.

START

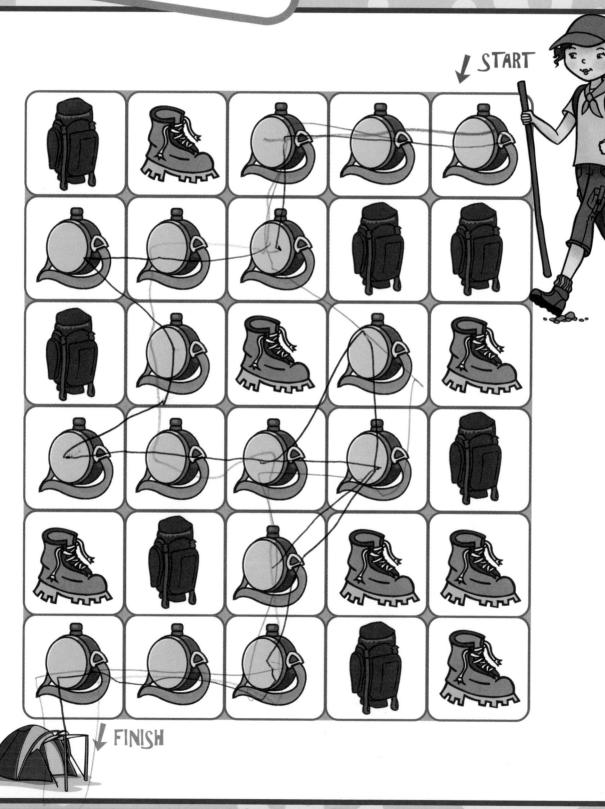

FINISH

Answer on page 284

Recipes

PERFECT PB&J PINWHEELS

Snacks

PB&J pinwheels are perfect for parties! Serve these on a platter and watch your friends gobble 'em up! Or, pack them in your lunch for a different way to eat your PB&J.

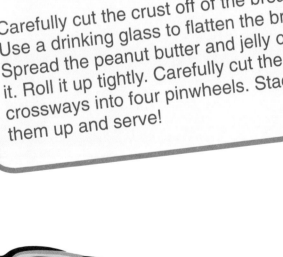

INGREDIENTS & DIRECTIONS

You'll need:

- Peanut Butter
- Jelly
- Whole wheat bread

Carefully cut the crust off of the bread*. Use a drinking glass to flatten the bread. Spread the peanut butter and jelly onto it. Roll it up tightly. Carefully cut the roll crossways into four pinwheels. Stack them up and serve!

*Ask your parents if you have any allergies.

Dress Styles
Glamour
TIPS

Body shapes come in a lot of different sizes, but everyone can look super cute with these dress style tips! Find the best dresses for your body type and you'll be stylin'.

Best For Straight

You might have a "straight" body type if...you have a petite frame, with relatively small top and bottom body shape, with very little curves.

Look for sweetheart-style necklines and draped pockets to add soft curves to your figure.

Best For Pear

You might have a "pear" body type if...you have a bottom heavy shape; narrow shoulders; and larger lower hips and thighs.

Wear intricate details on your top—like small buttons, lace, or roses—to keep the focus on your upper body.

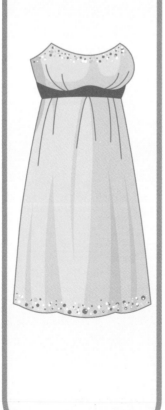

Best For Curvy

You might have a "curvy" body type if...you have a top and bottom heavy body shape,

Curvy girls look great in V-neck tops that accentuate their waist.

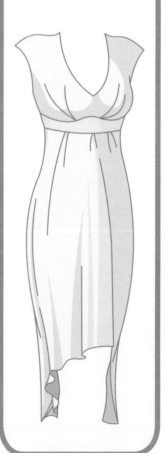

Best For Athletic

You might have an "athletic" body type if...you have broad, sporty shoulders; defined arms; toned tummy; and square hips.

Show off your toned and fit arms with a one shoulder dress.

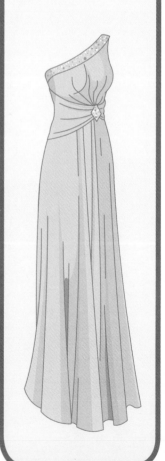

Design your own dress! Use this page to design your ideal dress that fits your body type—and most importantly, fits your personality!

FANCY RESTAURANT

Fill in the blanks to complete this silly story about going to a fancy restaurant. Pick a NOUN, ADJECTIVE, or VERB from the word bank to place in a corresponding blank, or think of your own weird words!

One of my _Cranky_ [ADJECTIVE] things to do is go on a trip to a fancy

restaurant. Sometimes there are _Dessert_ [NOUN] s on the table and it

looks so _heavy_ [ADJECTIVE]. After I _Slurp_ [VERB] my food, I _Fly_ [VERB]

a tasty soda or juice. After a bit, the _Pencil_ [NOUN] brings my

Waiter [NOUN]. It's absolutely _Frightening_ [ADJECTIVE] Next comes the best part—

headban [NOUN]! It's always fun _Crunch_ [VERB] ing at a fancy restaurant.

WORD BANK

ADJECTIVES
favorite
pretty
delicious
grassy
~~cranky~~
ugly
~~heavy~~
mean
frightening

NOUNS
candle
frog
~~waiter~~
meal
~~dessert~~
bug
~~pencil~~
headband
earring

VERBS
order
drink
~~slurp~~
eat
crunch
cry
crash
play
fly

Party ANiMaLS

Are you a super seeker? Put your eyes to the test and see if you can find 10 differences between the picture on the top and the one on the bottom.

Answer on page 284

What Kind of Wild Cat Are You Most Like?

Lion • Tiger • Jaguar

1. How would you describe your group of friends?
- **a –** A large group of people with all different sorts of personalities and interests. (1)
- **b –** On the small side and mostly interested in the same things. (2)
- **c –** High-energy and extremely motivated. (3)

2. What's your favorite thing to do when you feel like being lazy?
- **a –** Soak up some sun! (3)
- **b –** Go for a relaxing swim. (2)
- **c –** Nap! (1)

3. Do you exercise?
- **a –** Sure, it's part of staying in shape. (2)
- **b –** Only when I have to… (1)
- **c –** It's one of my favorite things to do! (3)

4. Which class office would you most likely run for?
- **a –** President, obviously! (1)
- **b –** Vice President or Treasurer—I don't want too much of the spotlight. (2)
- **c –** Events Coordinator—I like being behind the scenes. (3)

5. When are you most active or motivated?
- **a –** In the morning and for most of the afternoon. (3)
- **b –** From late afternoon to the early evening. (2)
- **c –** At night. (1)

6. What do you like most about yourself?
- **a –** My focus and strength—once I commit to something, I make sure it gets done! (2)
- **b –** My courage and ability to organize other people. (1)
- **c –** My energy and williigness to work on many different things at once. (3)

Lion 6-9 points

You are most like a lion! You are real leadership material and have a big network of friends and people who look up to you. Nothing phases you!

Tiger 10-14 points

You are most like a tiger! You always get the job done, even if you're working alone. Never underestimate your ability to achieve a goal.

Jaguar 15-18 points

You are most like a jaguar! You have so much energy, both physically and when it comes to doing all sorts of things at once. You are unstoppable!

Sudoku
BATHING BEAUTY

Pretend you're on the beach and try to decode this sudoku. Fill in the empty squares so that each row, column, and square contains the numbers 1–9 only once.

			8				2	
3		4		9		8		5
9		2					4	
	3	6		4				
	4		2	7				
5	2						3	
	5		3		9	6	7	
2				6			1	9
6		8				3		

Word Warrior

From books to magazines to websites and beyond, words are everywhere! Complete these wordy lists — the answers may surprise you!

 What is your favorite magazine?

 What book(s) have you read more than once?

 Who is your favorite author?

What do you like to read at the beach?

 What is your favorite website?

How To TIPS

Every friendship has its ups and downs, but if it is real friendship, you will be able to make up after a fight and be even better friends than you were before. Use the following suggestions to avoid problems with your best buds.

Keep Your BFs Forever

DON'T TEASE!

Teasing is terrible! It makes anyone, no matter how popular or unpopular, feel awful. But sometimes kids will do things because of peer pressure.

CONFRONT YOUR TEASERS

If one of your good buds suddenly starts teasing you with a bunch of other girls, chances are she felt pressured to do so. Go talk to your pal and tell her how she hurt your feelings.

DON'T BE A BLABBERMOUTH!

Friends tell each other everything including top-secret secrets! When your best bud confides in you, never tell her secret to anyone else. Blabbing would be the quickest way to lose your pal's trust.

KEEP SECRETS!

You know that you can tell your best bud anything and she won't tell anyone else. If you absolutely cannot keep a secret to yourself, confide in a diary so that no one else will see.

BROKEN PROMISES

What should you do if you suspect that a friend has spilled one of your secrets and broken a promise? Calmly ask her. If she says she didn't tell anyone, stop and think if maybe someone overheard.

CUT LOOSE BAD FRIENDS

If you find out that she did spill the beans, you may want to think twice about telling her your secrets. There's no point hanging out with someone who makes you feel bad. You're worth having good friends!

SUPERSTAR

Superstars love to sing and dance the night away! Find these words about superstars in the word search below. Look up, down, backward, forward, and diagonally.

| Band | Crowd | Glitter | Microphone | Sing |
| Costume | Dance | Makeup | Popular | Voice |

```
E M M S X G N L I T A B T B
O P M V I L N P H T O U G E
T U T H T I E E H A B P S S
B O E M U T S O C R O W D C
D D G I J T I D V I P M A F
S E E C F E N M R T O E N I
E S Z R I R G K D R T V C H
R C P O P U L A R A Y N E G
M E P P F G C I A V T E E N
C H E H M G O R U I E I D G
F G Y O N N A X E M L A R L
E R E N C O Y N A E P M N N
G P U E K A M M J D N A B W
R G T C T O P E N T S R N E
```

Answer on page 285

DENIM DIVA

Denim duds are a quick way to look chic. Can you find the two pictures that are exactly alike?

Answer on page 285

Let's Draw an
Emperor Penguin Chick

On a separate piece of paper, follow these simple steps using a pencil and an eraser.

1 Penguins start out life pretty fluffy. First, sketch out these three shapes. It will look like a snowman.

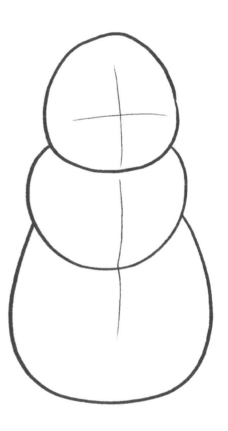

2 Next, sketch in the wings and rough shapes for its eyes, beak, and toes.

3 Now, add some detail to its face, then some pencil marks to indicate its fluffy feathers.

4 Add some shading and this little penguin is all set to waddle around.

Fairy Castle Maze

Follow the path from **Start** to **Finish** to go from the bottom of the castle to the tiara.

FINISH

START

Answer on page 285

Outer Space

Using the pictures below, complete this rebus puzzle about outer space.

____ ____ ____ ____ ____ ____ ____ ____ ____ ____ ____ ____

Doodlin' >>>>>>>>>>>>>>>>>>>>>>>>>>>
Hip Purses

Use your imagination to finish details for this purse collection.

Write Your
Own Story

Get inspired and write your own story about your ideal pet.

If I could have any pet, I'd like to have...

Recipes

• • •

POPCORN PARADISE
Snacks

Trail mix is an easy treat for you to grab when you're on the go. It's packed with healthy bits of nuts and dried fruit to keep busy girls like you satisfied between meals!

INGREDIENTS & DIRECTIONS

You'll need:

- Air-popped popcorn

- Peanuts (or any of your favorite nuts)

- Dried fruit (like banana chips, dried pineapple, and raisins)

- Cinnamon

Combine popcorn,* nuts, and dried fruit in an airtight container. Sprinkle with cinnamon. Close lid and shake, shake, shake!

*Ask your parents if you have any allergies.

CAMPING TRIP

Fill in the blanks to complete this silly story about a camping trip. Pick a NOUN, ADJECTIVE, or VERB from the word bank to place in a corresponding blank, or think of your own weird words!

Every year, my family goes on a big camping trip. Everyone

brings _____ing bags and a _____, and we
         [VERB]   [NOUN]

_____ everything over the fire. My _____ things
    [VERB]   [ADJECTIVE]

to do are _____ing and canoeing. At _____,
             [VERB]   [NOUN]

we sit around the fire and tell _____ stories. It's always
                                  [ADJECTIVE]

funny to see who gets the most afraid! When it's time to leave the

camp _____, everyone is _____—camping is
        [NOUN]   [ADJECTIVE]

one of our favorite things to do!

WORD BANK

ADJECTIVES
favorite   feathery
scary   flat
sad   slimy
crunchy   fluffy
huge

NOUNS
tent   circus
site   dog
night   purse
bird   blanket
dawn

VERBS
sleep   sing
fish   email
cook   climb
smell   paint
cough

How Do You Deal with the Unexpected?

LIKE ME   NOT LIKE ME

1. I get ready for school the night before—pack my lunch, get my outfit together, etc.

2. I hate horror or suspense movies!

3. Pop quiz? No big deal!

4. I blush very easily.

5. I don't mind when I'm called on in class, even if I'm focused on doodling on my notebook.

6. My friends always let me know about weekend plans way in advance.

7. I like to read books without knowing what they're about.

8. If I get an unexpected call from my crush, I definitely won't come to the phone!

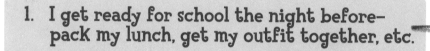

238

9. I like to shop for whatever reason—I don't need to have a specific thing in mind.

10. The idea of a surprise party terrifies me!

11. If a classmate cancels on a meeting for a project, I just try to reschedule.

12. On the first day of school, if my classes aren't exactly what I picked, you can find me sorting things out in the office.

13. My soccer coach Know I'm happy playing anywhere on the field.

14. I'm an understudy for the lead role in the school play...but I really hope no one gets sick before opening night!

15. My favorite Kind of party is a surprise party, of course!

Tally it up!

If you chose mostly "Like Me" answers, you are great at handling the unexpected! You're as cool as a cucumber. You can really roll with the punches.

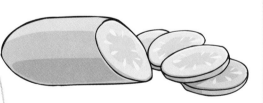

If you chose mostly "Not Like Me" answers, you'd rather know about something in advance than be surprised! You're an excellent planner, but sometimes that means you get caught up in events.

Diva Dos and Don'ts
Glamour TIPS

Everyone likes to be a diva once in a while! But what separates a girl from a diva? Check it out!

DIVA DO

- Apply lip gloss!
- Spend time applying the right make-up!
- Wear cute hair clips!
- Dress like a rock star!
- Wear different color shirt and pants!
- Play a sport!
- Know the hottest new pop stars!

DIVA DON'T

- Apply lip gloss sloppily!
- Wear too much make-up!
- Wear messy ponytails!
- Dress like their teacher!
- Wear the same colors all the time!
- Ever, ever diet!
- Forget who they are!

QUICK DIP

Search, find, and circle these 10 things.

Beach balls (2)   Green bikini   Polka-dot bikini
Clown   Mohawk   Softball
Flower   Penguin   Turtles (2)
Pink dress

Answer on page 286

READY FOR SCHOOL

Use the clues about school supplies to complete this crossword puzzle.

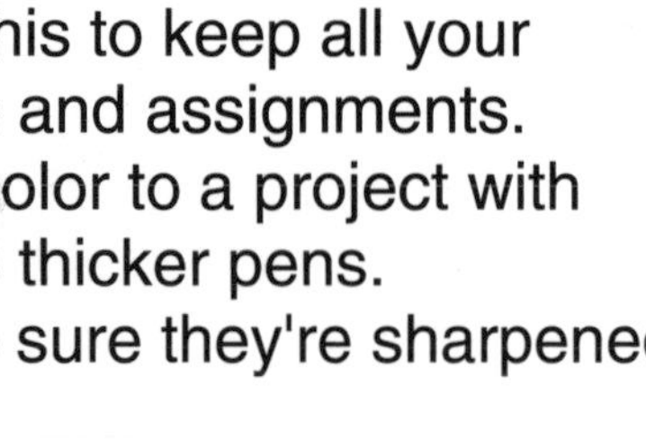

ACROSS

1. The yummiest part of the school day.
4. Use it to measure stuff.
6. Write notes on _________.
7. They're used in art class to cut things.
8. Read these during school.

DOWN

2. Use this to keep all your dates and assignments.
3. Add color to a project with these thicker pens.
5. Make sure they're sharpened.

Answer on page 286

List your

Chill Out

From snowflakes to snow boots, winter is tough to beat in terms of frosty fun! Create a list of wintry cool things to do and wear.

What kind of hat do you wear in wintertime?

What do you look forward to when it snows?

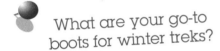
What are your go-to boots for winter treks?

What are you favorite toasty treats?

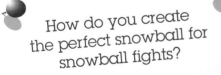
How do you create the perfect snowball for snowball fights?

Tennis Maze

Hip, hip, hooray! Help this girl get to the end of the tennis court by following the correct path through the maze. The correct path is made up of tennis balls only.

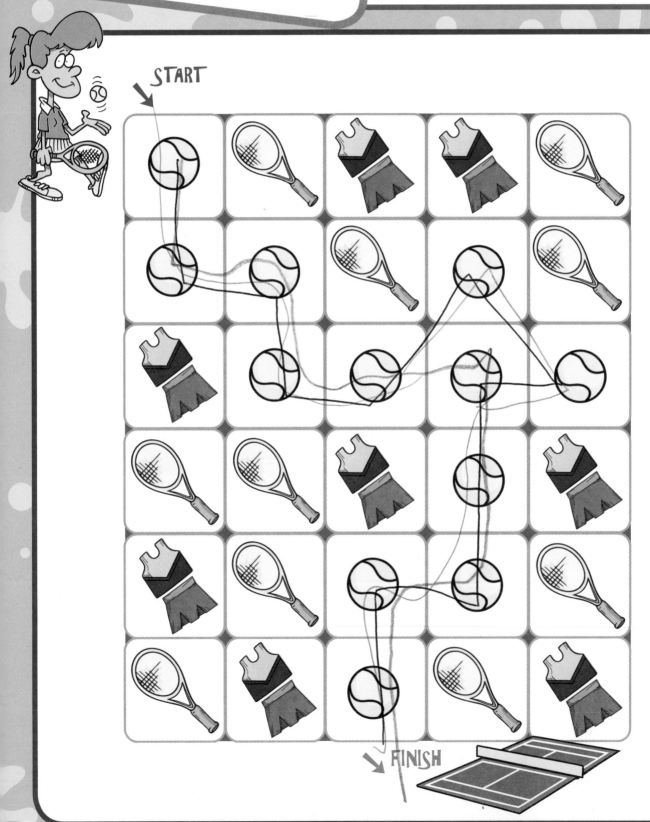

START

FINISH

Answer on page 286

Sudoku
SUMMER SUN

Kick back and relax with this sudoku. Fill in the empty squares so that each row, column, and square contains the numbers 1–9 only once.

	5		7					
		1		6		2		
4		6		8		1		3
	8	2		7	4		3	
	6		8			7		4
9	4		3	5		8		6
7			5			3	4	
		5		4		6		2
	1		2	3			8	9

Twinkling Tiara

Using the pictures below, complete this rebus puzzle about someone who would wear a tiara.

- SENT +

(handwritten: Present)

(handwritten: Bottle) - BO - LE + Y

(handwritten: frely)

+ - DRE

(handwritten: Presly)

_ _ _ _ _ _

_ _ _ _ _ _

Precious Pearls

Are you a super seeker? Put your eyes to the test and see if you can find 10 differences between the picture on the top and the one on the bottom.

Answer on page 287

CATWALK

You can always see the latest fashion on catwalks. Find words about catwalks in the word search. Look up, down, backward, forward, and diagonally.

Celebrity	Cool	High heels	Model	Strut
Clothes	Fashion	Makeup	Runway	Walk

```
F Z E T D I N S M I S A P N
O P P T O I R W C O G M O K
M T I R S Z O A O P D I U F
A I R W E D D L O Y H E S J
K K R P E S A K L S K T L E
E M A C A Z E B A O R T E D
U P V D F N E F M U M M E W
P I N O S M A O T U E O H R
R G D A T H X D R B Q E H U
L H N C L O T H E S R X G N
R R Y R I E Z F E A Z T I W
F R S L E K D E P F W R H A
E O H L S S E F N S E R D Y
T C E L E B R I T Y P T H X
```

ICE-CREAM PARLOR

Fill in the blanks to complete this silly story about the ice cream parlor. Pick a NOUN, ADJECTIVE, or VERB from the word bank to place in a corresponding blank, or think of your own weird words!

I got a summer job at the ice cream parlor. Every day,

lots of _____s come in to cool off and _____
        [NOUN]   [VERB]

a tasty treat. We sell _____s with one, two, or three scoops.
                       [NOUN]

My job is to scoop whatever _____ flavor a customer
                            [ADJECTIVE]

wants and put it in a _____ cone. Sometimes we get so
                      [ADJECTIVE]

_____ that the line goes out the _____. On break,
[ADJECTIVE]   [NOUN]

everyone who is _____ing gets to _____ a scoop.
                [VERB]   [VERB]

I love working at the ice cream parlor!

WORD BANK

ADJECTIVES

crispy
busy
yummy
salty
weird
ugly
giggly
steamy
sharp

NOUNS

customer
door
cone
lamp
notebook
beach ball
airplane
camera
carpet

VERBS

eat
work
try
cry
throw
crush
scoop
twirl
sling

249

How To TIPS
Be More Assertive

You may think that you're the only one who feels shy when speaking in class or talking to someone new. But you're not! If sometimes you are too timid to get your ideas across, consider these helpful hints.

KEEP A JOURNAL

Oftentimes, expressing yourself to others is difficult because you don't know exactly how you feel. Keeping a journal will help reveal your thoughts and organize your ideas.

THINK IT THROUGH

Do you find yourself afraid to speak up in class or add to a discussion? Take a moment to think through your ideas before speaking. This will give you time to organize your thoughts.

VALUABLE THOUGHTS

Keep in mind that your thoughts are original and valuable. Friends, family, and teachers want to know what you think and where you stand on issues.

ACCEPT A COMPLIMENT

Pay attention to your reaction to compliments. You may find that you explain them away or downplay them. The next time you receive a compliment say, "Thank you."

THANKS

Never underestimate the power of practice. Do you have to deliver an oral report in front of your class? Don't be embarrassed to practice it in front of your family or close friend. Imagining yourself in a positive situation will help you feel more comfortable.

PRACTICE

ACCEPT YOURSELF

Not everyone is a chatterbox. Realizing that you are quiet is the first step toward accepting yourself. Once you are comfortable with yourself, you'll begin feeling more comfortable around other people.

Write Your Own Story

Get inspired and write your own story about your favorite designer labels.

Some of my favorite designer labels are...

?

If I Ruled the World

What would you do if you ruled the world? It's fun to dream big and fantasize about interesting things! Use your imagination to answer these just for fun questions.

If you were president, what would you do to make the world a better place?

If you could live anywhere on Earth, where would you live?

If you could switch places with someone for a day, who would it be?

If you could have dinner with one living person, who would it be?

If you could change one thing about your personality, what would it be?

Top 3 Fashion Glamour TIPS

It's easy to incorporate fashion into your life—and your wardrobe. Follow these top 3 tips and you'll be well on your way.

Fashion Tip #1

Adding a simple accessory will finish your look and make you more polished. Try:

- Belt
- Scarf
- Hat
- Pair of earrings

Fashion Tip #2

Clean your closet! It's always good to do this at least once a season. Try:

- Tossing everything you haven't worn for a year
- Organizing sweaters, skirts, pants, and dresses by color—darkest to lightest
- Tucking your coats away for the summer to make room for your new sundresses

Fashion Tip #3

Shop till you drop! Here's how to do it successfully. Try:

- Bringing a friend with you—get opinions.
- Different outfits. It's a good way to experiment with new styles.
- Knowing your budget and staying within it.

Whether long and dangly or short and sweet, earrings are a great complement to any outfit. Can you find the two pictures that are exactly alike?

Roller Skate Maze

She's a whiz on her wheels! Help this roller skater get to the disco ball by following the correct path through the maze. The correct path is made up of roller skates only.

START ↓

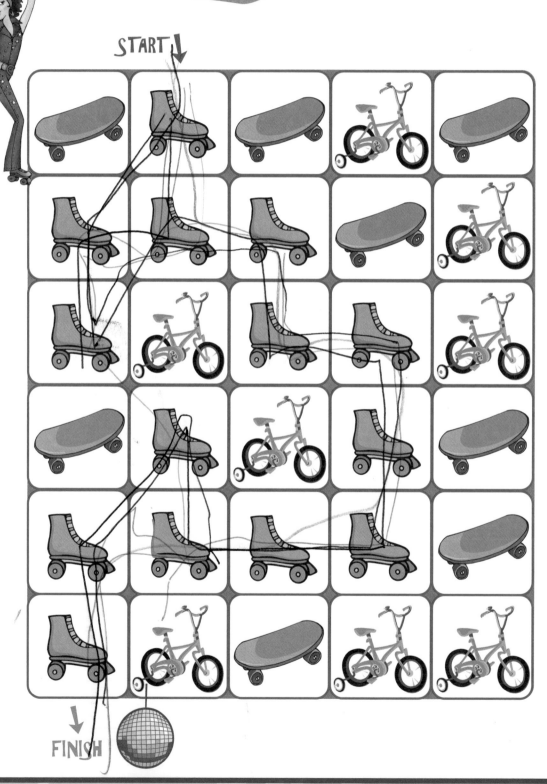

FINISH ↓

Answer on page 288

Which *Hairstyle* Should You Try?

Follow this chart to find out which hairstyle suits you. At the end, you'll find a 'do that just might be perfect for you!

Start

How long does it take to style your hair?
- Wash and go!
- 30 minutes!
- Forever!

What kind of product do you use?
- Wild hair can't be tamed!
- Leave-in conditioner

What do you mostly use your phone for?
- Play games
- Phone calls
- Text message

What's your favorite sleepover activity?
- Take tons of quizzes
- Prank call cute boys

What's your most comfy style?
- Cargo pants and t-shirt
- Cute dress

How big is your brush?
- Large
- Small

What do you normally talk about?
- Friends
- Boys

SOFT, WAVY, AND NATURAL
This style reflects your laidback personality and natural beauty.

HIGH PONYTAIL
Fun and flirty, this hairstyle is so you!

CHIC UP 'DO
You're a fashionista who is always on trend. Try a messy bun or a stylish French twist to accessorize and you'll always look glam.

BEST DAY EVER

Fill in the blanks to complete this silly story about the best day ever. Pick a NOUN, ADJECTIVE, or VERB from the word bank to place in a corresponding blank, or think of your own weird words!

On my best day ever, I wake up to the smell of _____
[NOUN]

cooking downstairs. In my _____ slippers and _____,
[ADJECTIVE]   [NOUN]

I go downstairs to _____. Soon, my friends call and invite me
[VERB]

to a concert. I go pick out my favorite outfit before leaving my house.

The day is so _____, so _____ing my bike is extra
[ADJECTIVE]   [VERB]

_____! When I meet up with my friends, we plan how the
[ADJECTIVE]

rest of the day will go. Once the _____ starts, we all start to
[NOUN]

_____! This really was one of the best days ever!
[VERB]

WORD BANK

ADJECTIVES
bacon
robe   volleyball
music   telephone
movie   hamster
swimsuit   diary

NOUNS
comfy   stormy
beautiful dark
fun   cute
difficult sleek
snowy

VERBS
eat   hiccup
pedal   sing
hold   smell
shiver   draw
sleep

Doodlin' Space Cadet

>>>>>>>>>>>>>>>>>>>>>>>>>>

Use your imagination to finish designing the wardrobe and accessories for this space collection.

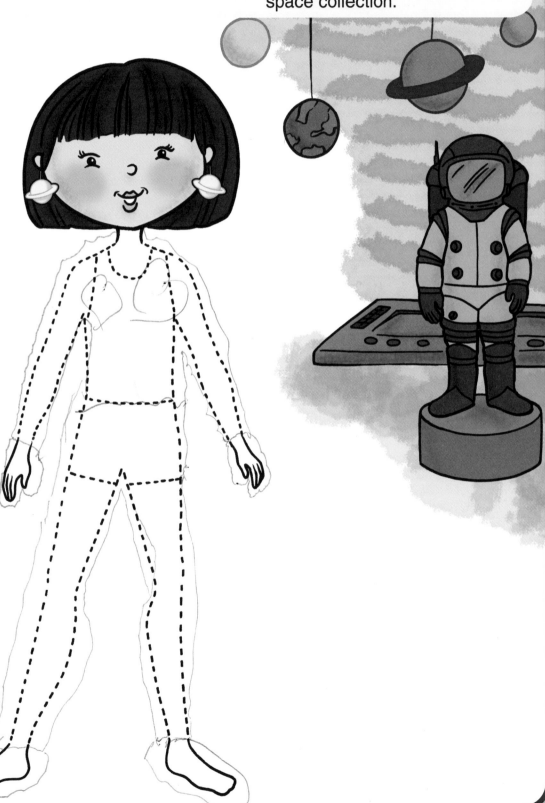

• List your Dream Big, Girlfriend!

It's never too late to map out your future. Now's the time to make a list of milestones of where you want to be in your life. Make sure to dream big, girlfriend!

What do you want to do in the next year?

What do you want to do in twenty years?

What do you want to do in five years?

What do you want to do in fifty years?

What do you want to do in ten years?

Love Your Beautiful Skin

Glamour TIPS

A clear complexion is easy to pull off. Just follow these simple tips and you'll be on your way to loving your clean, clear, and beautiful skin!

SQUEAKY-CLEAN!

Wash your face with a gentle cleanser every night before you go to bed. Dirt, make-up gunk, and bacteria cause breakouts. Make sure your skin is spotless before you turn in for your beauty sleep.

HEALTHY GLOW

Stay smooth and soft by using an oil-free moisturizer after cleansing your skin.

RADIANT REST

Speaking of beauty sleep... get lots of it! Getting enough rest helps your skin renew itself, so it always looks bright and fresh.

SPLISH SPLASH

Drink lots of water so you're staying healthy from the inside out.

PROTECT AND PAMPER

Don't forget your sunscreen! Make this a regular step in your clean and clear skincare routine.

Recipes

• • • LEMON-LIME RASPBERRY SODA

Snacks

This make-it-yourself soda includes frozen raspberries—a healthy, refreshing alternative to sugary store-bought soda. Plus, it looks oh-so-pretty!

INGREDIENTS & DIRECTIONS

You'll need:

- Seltzer water
- 2 lemons
- 2 limes
- Handful of raspberries

Pop the raspberries* in the freezer a few hours before serving soda. While raspberries are freezing, pour seltzer water into 2 glasses. Carefully cut lemons and limes in half. Squeeze the lemons and limes into the seltzer water. Take the raspberries out of the freezer and drop them into the glasses—they'll keep the seltzer nice and cool!

Makes 2 glasses

*Ask your parents if you have any allergies.

Write Your
Own Story

When it comes to book smarts, I'm especially great at...

?

What's Your Signature Hairdo?

It's always fun to change up how you look. Take this quiz to find out which hairstyle would look good on you. Even if it's something different, it doesn't hurt to try something new!

Updo • Curly • Straight

1. What's your favorite thing at an amusement park?
- a – Roller coaster (2)
- b – Bumper cars (3)
- c – Midway games (1)

2. The school dance is tomorrow night—what are you wearing?
- a – A print skirt and a cute top. (3)
- b – A solid colored dress with ruffles. (1)
- c – A bright, fun dress. (2)

3. What kind of car would your future, dream car be?
- a – Something small, cute, and zippy! (1)
- b – A sports car. (2)
- c – A convertible. (3)

4. What would your ultimate concert experience be like?
- a – On the small side so everyone can chat about the music between songs. (1)
- b – Loud, with everyone dancing! (2)
- c – Something laid back, and hopefully outdoors. (3)

5. If you could have any of these house pets, which would you choose?
- a – A dog. (2)
- b – A fish. (1)
- c – A cat. (3)

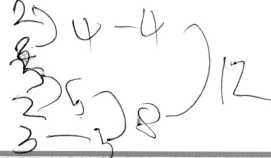

Updo 5-8 points

If you scored 5 to 8 points, your perfect hairstyle is an updo. You're an organized kind of person. Creating an updo will keep things in place, but still look super cute.

Curly 9-11 points

If you scored 9 to 11 points, your perfect hairstyle is curly or wavy. You enjoy fun, sometimes unexpected things, and your hair should show that!

Straight 12-15 points

If you scored 12 to 15 points, your perfect hairstyle is sleek or straight. You're easy-going and relaxed. Let your hair down and give it lots of shine.

How To TIPS

Celebrate your friendships by being together and sharing good times. Make a super cool autograph book so you can keep all your friends' signatures for when they're famous!

Awesome Autograph Book

GET CRAFTY

You can buy an autograph book but it's even more fun to make it yourself! It can be a couple of sheets of colored paper stapled together. Or, you can go all out and buy special supplies from a craft store.

BRIGHT AND SHINY

Decorate your book using a combination of brightly colored markers, gel pens, glitter pens, stickers, photographs, and drawings to create an awesome album that you'll cherish for years to come.

FILL 'ER UP!

Be sure to take your autograph book with you to school, athletic events, gymnastics practice, ballet class, camp, or any other place you'll find a friend. Perhaps your parents would even let you invite your friends over for an autograph-signing party.

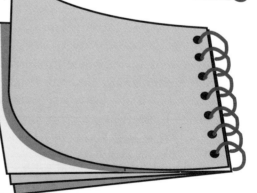

• List your

Dream Team

Do you remember your dreams when you wake up? Now's the time to write down your most memorable dreams.

 The scariest dream I have ever had was…

 My friends that appear in my dreams the most are…

The dream that embarrassed me the most was…

Family members that appear in my dreams the most are…

The place I dream about most often is…

Zzzz…

Answers

Page 5
Types of Hairstyles

Bob	Curled	Long	Pixie	Short
Crimped	Layered	Perm	Shag	Updo

```
R C X A E K L E E E J L X L
J R I C T A E S C H Q B X U
U I F X Y P E S H U F W L U
P M B E U O S N G A Z D G P
B P R I Z M N N V E G U Y D
V E S A B F O P O C I P S O
D D I N B L Y J R C G E H Q
Z L N X A S U W Y E V W W T
A B J H I F B U Z O A X S R
L L B Q T P V A F M M V Q O
B Q Q W D R P U H U V R A H
B R G L Z I S C I N R R L S
D L Y D D E L R U C R F V D
P E R M D T R O E Z C X H G
```

Page 9
Kitten Maze

Page 11
Rock and Roll

Page 13
Hip, Hop, Hooray!

JUMP ROPE

Answers

Page 16
Dancing Queen

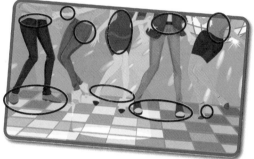

Page 22
Rockin' Tunes

6	9	1	2	7	5	8	3	4
5	7	8	3	1	4	6	2	9
4	2	3	6	9	8	1	7	5
7	8	6	9	4	3	5	1	2
1	4	5	7	2	6	3	9	8
2	3	9	5	8	1	4	6	7
9	1	4	8	3	7	2	5	6
3	6	2	4	5	9	7	8	1
8	5	7	1	6	2	9	4	3

Page 24
Trip to the Mall

Start

Finish

Page 25
Fit and Fabulous

Aerobics	Cardio	Pilates	Stretching	Tennis
Bike	Dance	Run	Swim	Yoga

```
N Q R F C S A G O Y T I B H
F O F A E C U I L S E D S I
A L S A C E D Q S A B J P F
H O M S N R K C D T P D A D
W S E T A L I P G U I M G S
O V O C D B I K E R O P G T
H E O S O A N U R X M E D R
Y H T R O L B E A E A T A E
S B E S F W S O I E E B M T
T A N R Z Z F T U G C Z P C
P N N N G S G R R B A X R H
A H I W H T Y O D P Y F X I
J W S W I M K I L N N A Q N
R G P I M U Z O F D H D M G
```

269

Answers

Page 26
Precious Animals

DOWN
1 Name for a professional horse rider
2 Small horse
4 You put this seat on a horse
5 Put these black pieces on a horse's head
7 Female horse
8 Type of horse that looks hand painted
9 Popular horse race
10 Horse feed

ACROSS
3 Latin word for horse
6 Horses win these at racing competitions
7 Hair on the back of the neck
8 Another term for a "true bred" horse
10 You measure horses in
   "_____," not fingers

Page 28
Beauty Parlor

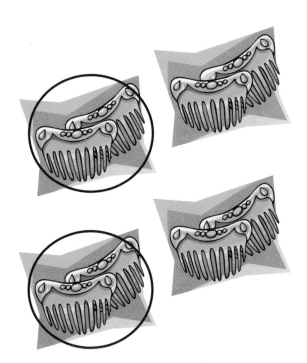

Page 29
Flower Shop

Page 31
Hairy Situation

Answers

Page 33
Trip to the Pet Shop

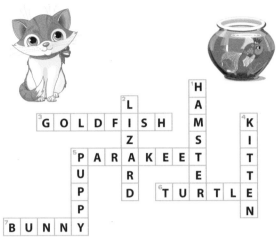

ACROSS
3. Orange-yellow aquarium dweller
5. Tiny, bright-colored parrot
6. Sometimes hides in its shell
7. Furry, with long ears

DOWN
1. Might run in a wheel
2. Small and scaly
4. Will grow up to chase mice
5. Baby version of "man's best friend"

Page 36
Wordsmith

| Book | Fiction | Non-fiction | Novella | Poem |
| Essay | Memoir | Novel | Play | Short story |

```
E P L H T P F R A E R S N R
I A Y L P O Y T T P E Y R E
B A F R O E Y A S S E D A E
B L R I O M E M L A V W N N
S L O D C T C D H P I G L I
R E I R I T S H I N M E S R
W V E T A C I T G S V K I W
E O C Q N E N O R O O T T H
E N O I T C I F N O N Y E I
N N U F T F Y O B M H A W B
A A S F O B P K H T Y S E F
J O S P N I E A L T A O F Y
T N C W C A Y N I B T U G A
D Q R P D Q T T M I F R R P
```

Page 38
Playground Paradise

M O N K E Y
B A R S

Page 39
Let's Play House Maze

Answers

Page 43
Flapper Girl

9	7	5	4	8	1	3	6	2
4	8	6	5	3	2	9	1	7
1	2	3	6	7	9	4	5	8
6	4	1	3	2	7	5	8	9
8	5	9	1	6	4	2	7	3
7	3	2	9	5	8	6	4	1
2	9	4	7	1	5	8	3	6
3	1	8	2	4	6	7	9	5
5	6	7	8	9	3	1	2	4

Page 47
Super Spacey

Page 48
Glamour Girl

Page 49
Flower Power

Answers

Page 51
High Heel Mania

Page 54
Candy Shop Maze

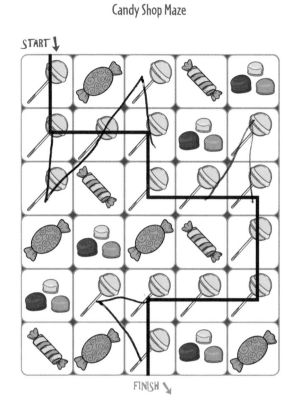

Page 61
Playing Dress Up

1	5	6	9	7	2	3	8	4
8	3	9	6	5	4	2	7	1
2	7	4	8	3	1	6	5	9
6	1	5	4	9	7	8	2	3
9	4	8	3	2	6	7	1	5
3	2	7	1	8	5	4	9	6
4	6	2	7	1	9	5	3	8
5	8	1	2	4	3	9	6	7
7	9	3	5	6	8	1	4	2

Page 63
Work of Art

| Carving | Drawing | Modern art | Painting | Sculpture |
| Ceramics | Exhibit | Mural | Portrait | Watercolor |

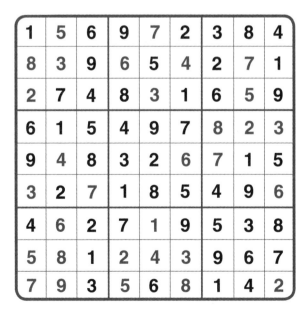

Answers

Page 64
Amazing Animals

ACROSS
3 Swings in a tree
4 Long neck
5 Big trunk
7 Slow moving, loves water

DOWN
1 White and furry
2 Lives in a hive
6 Striped cat
8 Big mane

Page 67
Something's Cookin'

Page 73
Fierce Manicure

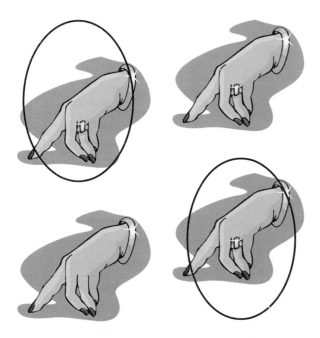

Page 74
Tea-Time

7	1	6	4	3	9	2	8	5
4	3	8	2	7	5	6	9	1
9	5	2	8	6	1	7	4	3
8	4	5	3	1	2	9	6	7
2	6	1	9	5	7	4	3	8
3	7	9	6	4	8	1	5	2
6	9	7	5	2	3	8	1	4
1	8	3	7	9	4	5	2	6
5	2	4	1	8	6	3	7	9

Answers

Page 75
City Living

Page 78
Trip to the Mall

Page 82
Penguin Maze

Page 83
Miss Fashionista

Answers

Page 84
Music Lover

Alternative	Dance	House	Pop	Reggae
Classical	Hip hop	Opera	Rap	Rock

```
K O F R K P A W S A E N M S
H L S R C C H O I C V L N M
N Z O E N O J Z N J I S T I
Y Q A P Z L E A N W T D M M
S S E W E C D D J J A O Y E
J R B S O R O Z V G N U I P
F A A E U E A G G E R I A N
S C P F R O Q M O E R H L
P G P S E H H Q X V T O C S
B W C L A C I S S A L C Y E
E Q P E S S P V E R A K E A
E C T V C X H P R O T C E O
J I E O G I O O R C P J H S
C O S D Y P P M Z X E J G M
```

Page 85
Sombrero

9	5	2	4	8	7	3	6	1
3	6	4	1	5	2	8	7	9
1	7	8	6	3	9	5	4	2
5	2	3	9	6	1	7	8	4
8	1	9	7	4	5	6	2	3
6	4	7	3	2	8	9	1	5
4	9	6	8	1	3	2	5	7
2	3	1	5	7	6	4	9	8
7	8	5	2	9	4	1	3	6

Page 86
Abracadabra!

-AZ-NE+ -ND-E

F+ -H+ -T+S

M A G I C A L
F A I R I E S

Page 89
Cool Girl

Athletic	Fashion	Fun	Hobbies	Smart
Confidence	Friends	Happy	Nice	Smile

```
I L S D O Z Q R K E O S I C
E L O S N Y F T E L I M S Y
Z E C N E D I F N O C A R K
K O W I W H S D N E I R F B
U L Z Q S N E L E H T T N H
Z R S I R W O Y I P E N O R
R P R E A E C I N E L U S Y
P E S E I B B O H R H E P U
X M I X O F R U J S T P V P
E R C K E E J W D D A C C S
I D Y M E O O O Q H Q F P S
Z F E O M C S H H Y V H D O
E C O M D S H G T N I J F N
U V D M R A B E C R N V N E
```

Answers

Page 90
Color Mania

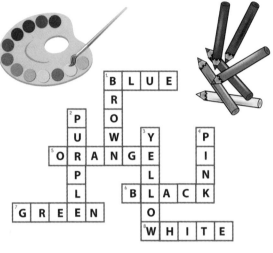

ACROSS
1. Color of the sky
5. Red + yellow = _____
6. All the colors mixed together make this
7. Color of the grass
8. Color of the clouds

DOWN
1. Color of chocolate
2. Red + blue = _____
3. Color of the sun
4. Shade of red

Page 93
Chick Flick

Page 94
Birthday Party Maze

Page 97
Love Song

Answers

Page 48
Puppies Galore

Bulldog	Papillon	Poodle	Puli	Spaniel
Husky	Pointer	Pug	Shih Tzu	Terrier

```
A A A T G O T R N T B J J D
H O P D O I E N E F N J S A
L N M L S F E S V E G N N I
I R A S E P W Z A Z S O O D I
V T H X C K N N S L D Q R A
H O I X N R M O L T L J H G
B T H N K G P I D H L O E J
R E T N I O P H I L U P L F
T R Z S P A N I E L B S L E
T R U E P O O D L E S K M
A I C C J D E G K F C A P Y
S E G U Q F N V U C M H V P
R R E N M M N E O P E F M Y
B M M H T U R S E S R T U I
```

Page 103
Flower Fun

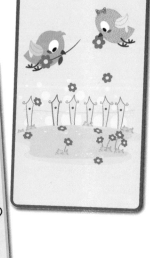

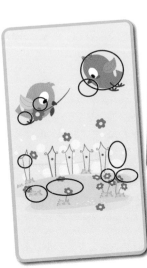

Page 107
Girl Talk

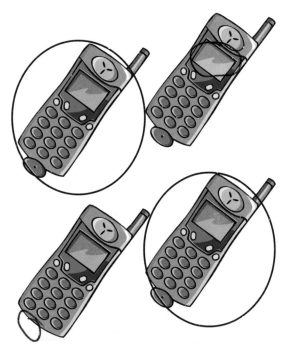

Page 112
Dude Ranch Maze

Answers

Page 113
Baseball Fun

9	8	7	5	3	2	1	4	6
6	2	5	7	4	1	9	8	3
4	1	3	6	9	8	2	7	5
5	9	8	1	6	4	3	2	7
2	4	1	3	7	9	5	6	8
3	7	6	2	8	5	4	9	1
7	6	9	4	1	3	8	5	2
8	3	2	9	5	6	7	1	4
1	5	4	8	2	7	6	3	9

Page 122
Makeup Glitz

ACROSS
1. Goes around the edges of your eyes
5. Color for your lips
6. Makes your lips shiny
8. Put this on your face with a fluffy pad

DOWN
2. Color for your eyelids
3. Goes on your eyelashes
4. Makes your cheeks rosy
7. Makes your skin soft and smooth

Page 123
Wedding Dress Styles

Ballerina	Column	Halter	Mermaid	Strapless
Bead	Empire	Lace	Princess	Sweetheart

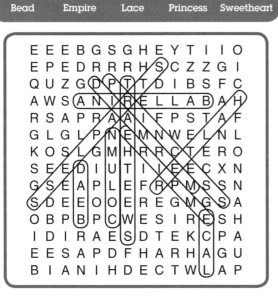

Page 124
Star Bright

279

Answers

Page 126
Prom Dress

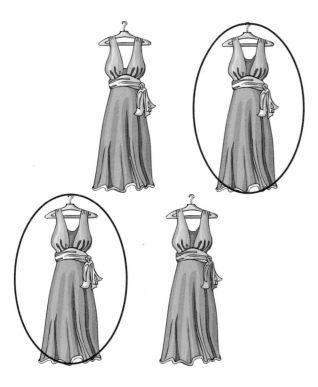

Page 127
Let's Fly

Page 128
Get Happy

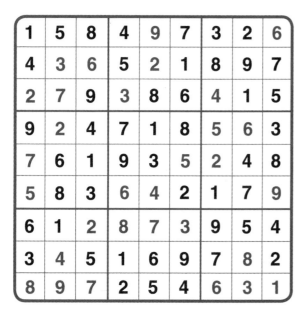

1	5	8	4	9	7	3	2	6
4	3	6	5	2	1	8	9	7
2	7	9	3	8	6	4	1	5
9	2	4	7	1	8	5	6	3
7	6	1	9	3	5	2	4	8
5	8	3	6	4	2	1	7	9
6	1	2	8	7	3	9	5	4
3	4	5	1	6	9	7	8	2
8	9	7	2	5	4	6	3	1

Page 131
Arts & Crafts Maze

Answers

Page 137
Ballet Star

Page 138
Cool Cats

Page 181
BFF Stuff

Page 182
Tropical Getaways

Aruba	Bali	Bora Bora	Fiji	Jamaica
Bahamas	Barbados	Curacao	Hawaii	Virgin Islands

```
A S R E T S C S E P I I J I
A N D C N N O S Y D T B F E
Z R Q N J D M H E S N T F E
S F O S A S A M A H A B C S
B M I B M L L K G H Z S Q T
S A R J A E S O Q B T L Y S
B A L X I R C I T L N J A D
B O R I C T O T N I I D T I
S K J E A A H B N J P M N K
R S S T C R W K A S G R Q J
N G I A M S Y W A B U R A Q
S I R A P I A S E G E E I S
H U T O D H E D C O C N S V
C U B O T J A O I D E E J S
```

Answers

Page 185
Last-Minute Groceries

Page 186
Unicorn Maze

Page 189
Winter Walk

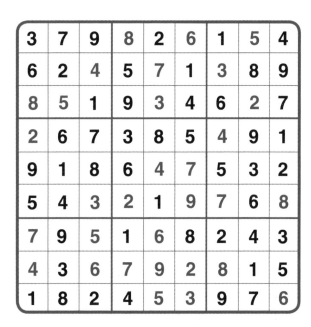

3	7	9	8	2	6	1	5	4
6	2	4	5	7	1	3	8	9
8	5	1	9	3	4	6	2	7
2	6	7	3	8	5	4	9	1
9	1	8	6	4	7	5	3	2
5	4	3	2	1	9	7	6	8
7	9	5	1	6	8	2	4	3
4	3	6	7	9	2	8	1	5
1	8	2	4	5	3	9	7	6

Page 191
Sunny Outlook

Answers

Page 199
Love Bug

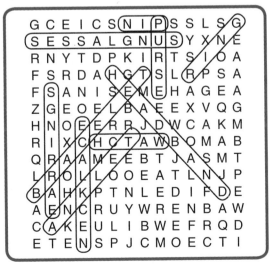

Page 203
Sweet Tooth

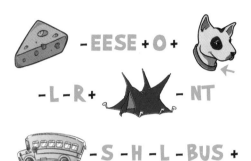

CHOCOLATE COOKIES

Page 204
Accessories

Anklet	Earrings	Necklace	Purse	Sunglasses
Bracelet	Headband	Pin	Ring	Watch

```
G C E I C S N I P S S L S G
S E S S A L G N U S Y X N E
R N Y T D P K I R T S I O A
F S R D A H G T S L R P S A
F S A N I S E M E H A G E A
Z G E O E L B A E E X V Q G
H N O E E R R J D W C A K M
R I X C H C T A W B O M A B
Q R A A M E E B T J A S M T
L R O L L O O E A T L N J P
B A H K P T N L E D I F D E
A E N C R U Y W R E N B A W
C A K E U L I B W E F R Q D
E T E N S P J C M O E C T I
```

Page 209
Rainbow Bright

Answers

Page 210
Party Fun

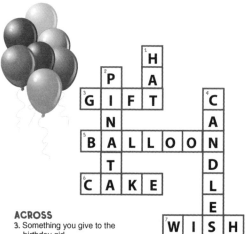

ACROSS
3. Something you give to the birthday girl
5. It's full of hot air.
6. You cover it with icing
7. Blow out the candles and make a _____.

DOWN
1. You wear it on your head
2. It's hung up with a string, and you hit it with a bat.
4. The number of _____ shows how old you are.

Page 215
Top Shops

Page 216
Hiking Trip Maze

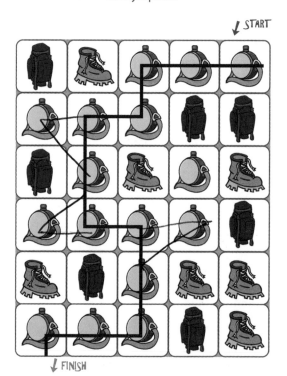

Page 221
Party Animals

Answers

Page 224
Bathing Beauty

7	6	5	8	3	4	9	2	1
3	1	4	7	9	2	8	6	5
9	8	2	6	5	1	7	4	3
8	3	6	1	4	5	2	9	7
1	4	9	2	7	3	5	8	6
5	2	7	9	8	6	1	3	4
4	5	1	3	2	9	6	7	8
2	7	3	5	6	8	4	1	9
6	9	8	4	1	7	3	5	2

Page 228
Superstar

Band   Crowd   Glitter   Microphone   Sing
Costume   Dance   Makeup   Popular   Voice

```
E M M S X G N L I T A B T B
O P M V I L N P H T O U G E
T U T H T I E E E H A B P S
B O E M U T S O C R O W D C
D D G I J T I D V I P M A F
S E E C F E N M R T O E N I
E S Z R I R G K D R T V C H
R C P O P U L A R A Y N E G
M E P P F G C I A V T E E N
C H E H M G O R U I E I D G
F G Y O N N A X E M L A R L
E R E N C O Y N A E P M N N
G P U E K A M M J D N A B W
R G T C T O P E N T S R N E
```

Page 229
Denim Diva

Page 232
Fairy Castle Maze

Answers

Page 233
Outer Space

-C -LE +

-STI + -BR -W

+A + -C

A S T R O N A U T

Page 241
Quick Dip

Page 242
Ready for School

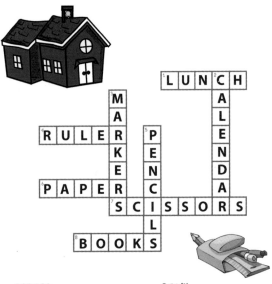

```
            ¹L U N C H
        ³M       A
        A        L
  ²R U L E R  ⁵P E N
        K     E    D
        E     N    A
  ⁶P A P E R  C
        S     I
     ⁷S C I S S O R S
              L
        ⁸B O O K S
```

ACROSS
1. The yummiest part of the school day.
4. Use it to measure stuff.
6. Write notes on _____.
7. They're used in art class to cut things.
8. Read these during school.

DOWN
2. Use this to keep all your dates and assignments.
3. Add color to a project with these thicker pens.
5. Make sure they're sharpened.

Page 244
Tennis Maze

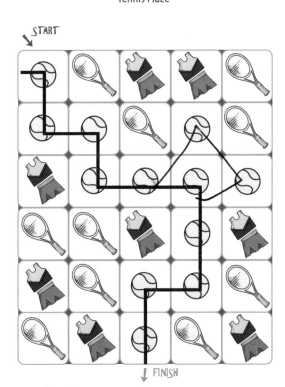

Answers

Page 245
Summer Sun

2	5	9	7	1	3	4	6	8
8	3	1	4	6	5	2	9	7
4	7	6	9	8	2	1	5	3
1	8	2	6	7	4	9	3	5
5	6	3	8	2	9	7	1	4
9	4	7	3	5	1	8	2	6
7	2	8	5	9	6	3	4	1
3	9	5	1	4	8	6	7	2
6	1	4	2	3	7	5	8	9

Page 246
Twinkling Tiara

- SENT +

- BO - LE + Y

+ - DRE

P R E T T Y
P R I N C E S S

Page 247
Precious Pearls

Page 248
Catwalk

2	5	9	7	1	3	4	6	8
8	3	1	4	6	5	2	9	7
4	7	6	9	8	2	1	5	3
1	8	2	6	7	4	9	3	5
5	6	3	8	2	9	7	1	4
9	4	7	3	5	1	8	2	6
7	2	8	5	9	6	3	4	1
3	9	5	1	4	8	6	7	2
6	1	4	2	3	7	5	8	9

Answers

Page 255
Awesome Earrings

Page 256
Roller Skate Maze